ADVENTURES
IN RISKY PLAY

What is your Yes?

by Rusty Keeler

Exchange Press

ISBN 978-0-942702-54-5

© 2020 Rusty Keeler

Book design by Scott Bilstad.

Editing by Tina Reeble and Erin Glenn.

Cover Photographs by Kisha Reid.

All photos © Rusty Keeler unless otherwise credited.

This book may not be reproduced in whole or in part by any means without written permission of the publisher.

For more information about other Exchange Press publications and resources for directors and teachers, contact:

Exchange Press
7700 A Street
Lincoln, NE 68510
(800) 221-2864
ExchangePress.com

This book is dedicated to you.

Contents

Background 6

PART 1
PLAY MANIFESTO 9

Play. 10
You Stop Play 14
Safety. 15
Risk vs Hazard. 17
Risky Play. 18
F.E.A.R. 21
Finding Your Yes 23
Licensor Censor. 26
This Book + You! 28

PART 2
WAYS TO SUPPORT RISKY PLAY 31

Childhood 33
Relationships with Your Children. 34
Trusting Children. 40
Risk-Benefit Analysis 45
Playwork 53
Rethink Your Rules 58
Environmental Choices. 61
Clothing. 67
Working with Parents. 70

PART 3
PROVOCATIVES. 72

The World is Upside Down. 75
Loose Parts 76
Stuff Says Yes 82
Hiding. 87
Fire 94
Water 102
Mud 109
Mud Kitchens 119
Bare Feet 125
A New Idea 128
Reclaiming Rules. 132
Rough and Tumble 137
Your Own "Anarchy Zone". 145
Chickens 148
Mixed-Age. 157
Sticks 165
Tree Climbing 169
Tools. 174
Licensing Perspective 1. 178
Licensing Perspective 2 180

PART 4
PROGRAM TOUR 183

Everybody Ready? 185
Nature Kindergarten, Scotland 186
Wild Woods, New Zealand 199
Adventure School, New York 204
Swedish Open-Air School. 212
Hudson Valley Sudbury School,
New York 216
Adventure Playgrounds 224
History 226
Contemporary
Adventure Playgrounds 232
Kolle 37, Germany 235
The Land, Wales 239
Rødovre Byggelegeplads
Adventure Playground, Denmark.... 242
The Venny Adventure Playground,
Australia. 246
Berkeley Adventure Playground,
California 250
Hands-On-Nature Anarchy Zone,
New York 254
Early Childhood Centers 258
Canterbury Community
Nursery School, Virginia 260
Takoma Park Cooperative
Nursery School, Maryland 264
Corner of the Sky, New York 268
Discovery Early Learning Center,
Maryland 272
Reimagining Recess 276
Conclusion..................... 283

PART 5
EXTRA STUFF.................... 285

Risk-Benefit Analysis Forms........ 286
End Notes 288
Resource List................... 290
Locations 291
About the Author 293

all life is change

times of change are opportunities to
change things for the better

we all have inner guidance that
begins in childhood and is with us today

this book is a conversation
with that part of yourself

breathe in the ideas

Background

My life in play and playscapes has led me to this point of reflection on children's play. After growing up with nature and an abundance of freedom I pursued a career in design which led me around the world. I began as a conceptual industrial designer for a playground equipment company where I learned both the importance of children's play and that I loved designing for play. The path took me to Europe where I was delighted and inspired by their philosophy of play and playgrounds—such thoughtful design and support for play. I returned home with new ideas and started my own business working with communities to design and build natural playscapes. I've written a couple of books you may know about, *Natural Playscapes* and *Seasons of Play*, that celebrate children's connections to nature and encourage you to build your own natural play spaces. Continuing to be inspired by play concepts of Europe I nurtured my love of adventure "junk" playgrounds and helped to start one in my hometown of Ithaca, NY. More recently, I co-founded the non-profit Just Play Project to promote child-friendly city initiatives that support all children's right to play. One of our projects was teaming up with our mayor to proclaim Ithaca, NY a "Free Range Kid City" supporting children's rights and engaging the conversation about children's play, equity, and mobility in our community.

On top of all that, and most importantly, I am the dad of two young children. That keeps me deeply in touch with play and connected to the heart space of the adult caregiver, trying my best and working to be better.

This book is a part of my journey, pondering play.

May it support your journey too.

PART 1

Play Manifesto

Play

Sunny summer day. Three preschoolers mix muddy sand in pots and pans, humming and chattering, adding water to soupy concoctions, pouring into frying pans and bowls, more stirring, concentrating, leaf-adding, serious looks and smiles.

Cold wintery day. Kindergarten children find ice in a bucket, try to get it out with sticks and shovels and by dumping the bucket over and jumping on top. The ice breaks and falls out. Children pick it up, drop it on the ground to watch it break into smaller pieces. Laughter. Then they jump on the broken ice bits.

Crisp fall day. School-age children balance on a large log. Each make their way across on their first try then begin to get a little silly and brave and try moving along the log in wilder ways. Hopping on one foot, running, walking sideways, walking backwards. Most make it. Some fall off.

Rainy warm spring day. The ground is saturated, puddles everywhere, toddlers in rain boots jumping and splashing. Laughter stops as a child slips and falls in a puddle. The wet child starts to cry. She gets up. Her friends come over to check on her. Her tears stop, then she gets right back to stomping through puddles.

Children at play. You have to love it. The beauty of human development right there in front of us. For as long as there have been humans there have been youngsters learning about themselves and the world around them through playful exploration. So many things happening at once. Imagination, imitation, investigation. Through play, children discover themselves and the world around them. Through play, they try out their skills and ideas, finding their strengths and limitations. Friendships are made, imaginary worlds created. Information is processed, skills develop. Laughter, tears, emotions, ideas… through play, a child explores what it is like to be human on our planet. The development of our species, the future adults and leaders of our world, all pass through the portal of a childhood that can create and lift who they are and who they become through the spirit and drive for play. We are wired for it. We are who we are because of how we played. And where we played. And with whom we played. What some disregard simply as "child's play" are actually some of the most important moments any of us will ever experience as we take this journey of life.

Play is a biological need and a necessity for healthy development. Freely chosen, child-directed play should be an unalienable right of all children everywhere. It should be supported, celebrated, honored, and allowed. We should listen to children. We should provide for their needs. We should work our hardest to support and lift up the beauty and wonder and wildness that is children's play.

PHOTO BY KISHA REID

Personally, play for play's sake has always been enough for me. Watching children find fuzzy caterpillars, or build a fort with branches, or slop around finger paint always seemed like the utmost important activity that a child could be doing. It doesn't really need labels or adult measures by which to prove that its existence is warranted or deemed necessary. It's necessary!

And yet, I also understand that in a modern world full of pressures and constraints on children's time in and out of school, something as obvious as play needs some scientific support and lobbying from adults who care enough to recognize that somehow, without us looking, good old-fashioned free play has been limited, sidelined, sublimated, and even decimated for way too many children in our busy, high-achieving, over-stimulated, over-scheduled, over-protected, overly biased, overly adult-oriented view of what children should be doing, accomplishing, competing and completing.

Childhood without access to free play has become a health crisis on too many fronts. First it was obesity for lack of movement. Then it was adult diseases moving down into childhood such as type II diabetes and heart disease because of poor diet and lack of exercise. And now, sad to say, schools are reporting that the levels of stress, depression, and anxiety among youths are at all-time highs. Mental health issues are becoming the number one problem reported by school district health professionals and they are desperate for solutions. Too many children are unable to face going to school and if they do make it there, they are barely able to function.

Many factors contributed to the loss and limitations of children's play: busy working parents, highly scheduled children's activities, performance pressures on schools to limit or cut recess, after-school programmed care, organizations' fear of liability and injuries, the lure of electronics and screen time, twenty-four hour news cycles and programmed television inducing fear in parents, and many other factors. For children of color, the pressures of racial bias and prejudice limit the freedom to play even more.[1] We know the lack of play is dire and if left unattended the results could be disastrous. Fortunately, we're attending to it!

So…to counter all these factors, sometimes we need to be able to scientifically back up the developmental need for play. Prove its point. Blind the people who don't understand yet with some science! There is an abundance of research on play and child development you can share with the people in power to make decisions to move the mountains (or mole hills) standing in the way of play. These people may be principals, teachers, early childhood professionals, school boards, camp directors, urban planners, parents, grandparents—even you.

As a start how about this list of play benefits published by the American Academy of Pediatrics[2]:

- It is through play that children at a very early age engage and interact in the world around them.

- Play allows children to use their creativity while developing their imagination, dexterity, and physical, cognitive, and emotional strength.

- Play is important to healthy brain development.

- Play allows children to create and explore a world they can master, conquering their fears while practicing adult roles, sometimes in conjunction with other children or a dult caregivers.

- As they master their world, play helps children develop new competencies that lead to enhanced confidence and the resiliency they will need to face future challenges.

- Undirected play allows children to learn how to work in groups, to share, to negotiate, to resolve conflicts, and to learn self-advocacy skills.

- When play is allowed to be child-driven, children practice decision-making skills, move at their own pace, discover their own areas of interest, and ultimately engage fully in the passions they wish to pursue.

- Ideally, much of play involves adults, but when play is controlled by adults, children acquiesce to adult rules and concerns and lose some of the benefits play offers them, particularly in developing creativity, leadership, and group skills.

- In contrast to passive entertainment, play builds active, healthy bodies.

- It has been suggested that encouraging unstructured play may be an exceptional way to increase physical activity levels in children, which is one important strategy in the resolution of the obesity epidemic.

- Perhaps above all, play is a simple joy that is a cherished part of childhood.

You don't need to know all the science of why play is vital for children's development to know that it is important stuff. Brain studies have proven its importance. Field research shows the bond between play, healthy development, and learning. Studies show time and again what we already know and believe: children need play. And they need lots of it.

One of the great things about supporting play is that it can be shown as a benefit to nearly all categories of childhood development and education. It's easy to make it fit any scenario. Is play good for literacy? Yes. Can it boost communication skills? Yes. Fight obesity? Yes. Can it stimulate science, technology, engineering, arts and math (STEAM) skills? Yes, yes, and yes. It fits whatever grant you might be writing, or whatever program you want to start. Play can support the goals of school districts, health departments, childcare center missions, YMCAs, after-school programs, parks, nature centers, science centers, and comprehensive plans for city centers. We can show the importance of play and how it enhances children's experiences and growth in all these various ways and environments.

Play rules!

Whenever I see children playing in rich, deep ways I feel happy and inspired. Being around play is fun and exciting and I marvel at it every time I see it. But it's not just the children doing the amazing stuff that gets to me. What also impresses me when I see this type of play are the adults who are permitting it. **Children will play whenever they can, but it's adults who determine if they get the chance.** It's adults who have the final say on when kids can play and what types of play they can engage in. It's adults who say yes and adults who say no. In one sense, it's sad. Adults hold all the power. Kids are ready to rock and roll and go for it and play away. But they really can only do so when an adult deems what they are doing is ok and says "yes" to play.

We know there is a lot of pressure on adults to do the right thing to keep kids safe and clean, and learning to become upright citizens. We know that it can be a stretch to say yes to some of kids' wilder play ideas. But adults are doing it. You're doing it. Whenever an adult is around play and children are doing amazing things it's because the adults have not said "no." And when an adult does not say no, they are in effect saying "yes" to play. And that's what this book is all about: **finding ways to say "yes" to children's play.**

You Stop Play

You love play. You champion it. You celebrate it. You support it! And yet, you may also stop it. Sometimes purposefully. Sometimes unwittingly.

All play has a beginning, middle, and end that children can decide on and play out for themselves. In free play children determine the content of their play and decide when it's finished or played out. **There is a natural flow that we can observe when children control their own play.** Adults who butt in take away that self-determination that children need as they grow, learn, and develop.

We may step in because something feels too dangerous. We may redirect to an activity that makes us feel more comfortable. We may stop the flow of play by jumping in ourselves to join the fun (without being invited). We may stop play by making suggestions to the play. Or narrating the play. Or applauding the play. The adults' voice can be a distraction. Saying "be careful" can be a dangerous distraction to a child who is concentrating on doing just that! We shift the focus from the pure play experience to the ever-watching adult-in-charge and what we think of the activity or moment. That's distractive and intrusive hovering (even if well-intentioned)!

We may stop play by trying to solve a difficulty that children may be having. We see a solution to a problem they seem to be having so we make a well-meaning suggestion. The children follow it and then it's done. But in doing so the adult robs the children of the opportunity to solve their own problems. Or let the problems be left unsolvable. As children try and fail, the problem-solving could flow into a whole different territory that we would never have imagined. The play story could continue in unexpected ways. *"If at first you don't succeed, try, try again"* is how the old saying goes, not *"if at first you don't succeed have an adult do it for you."* The solutions children come up with can be unexpected and amazing if we let them. If you can overcome the impulse to solve the problem it can be a fun and eye-opening experience to witness. Creative solutions can come from nowhere, or from trial and error, or children may shrug it off and switch to some other activity. It can be surprising for adults to see how little attachment children even have to getting a problem solved! We may think something is important to the children, only to realize that the children couldn't care less about actually solving the issue. For children's art and projects we often say "it's about process, not final product." The same goes for play. Even if they walk away. That's ok. "Teaching moments" are another adult construct that can stop play: adult agendas overpowering the children's agenda.

We stand up against racial and gender bias, but what about grown-up bias? Do children have rights? The right to play?

I say this all with love and support. But this book is meant to provoke. Push some buttons. Cross some boundaries. It's time to question some of our pre-conceived notions about the adult's role in children's play. And adults ruling children's play. It might get uncomfortable. It will definitely get messy. But if you can stick with me, I promise that exciting potential for positive change awaits. Read with an open heart. Take deep breaths as you go. *Don't worry: No children were harmed in the making of this book!*

Safety

Keeping children safe is one of the most important parts of our job as adults. Of course, we don't want anyone to get hurt. Not on our watch and not on anyone's watch. That's why there are rules and regulations. That's why you stay on your toes on the playground. That's why you're ever-vigilant: to keep disaster from happening. And that's a good thing. Let's start this section with that as a given.

Let's also keep things in perspective. Head injuries: bad. Death: really bad. Long bones broken: not great. Punctures and deep gashes: yuck, no thanks. But what about scratches? What about bruises? What about a head bonk or an ankle twist or a pinched finger? What about a bee sting? Questions for the philosophers, perhaps. But also for us.

What are your thresholds for smaller injuries? Where are your limits? What is acceptable risk and what is unacceptable? The edge between acceptable and unacceptable sets our course on how we patrol children's play. Of course every situation is different. Every child is different. Every family is different. Every program and school is different. The level of risk we accept for our own children may be much different than the level of risk we accept when we care for other people's children. That makes sense.

But what is meant by that old saying, "Better a broken bone than a broken spirit?" Does it mean that broken bones are ok? Or does it imply that a child's spirit could be damaged if we fixate soley on preventing injuries? Yes, I think that's it. I think it means we must trust children to make their own choices and test their own boundaries, and follow their own flights of fancy. Perhaps along the way they could get a bump, bruise, even a broken bone. But if they are free to experience it all and make decisions about how they want to be in the world then that is the true gift of childhood and the true gift of the adult caregiver—even though it could make the adult uncomfortable, and even if the child gets lightly injured. The consequences of stifling children and their play far outweigh the risks and results of a simple broken bone. A broken bone hurts. But a squashed spirit hurts more. Especially in the long run. Heavy stuff! Especially when you consider the squasher could be you.

Ouch! Now that hurts. Especially when all you're doing is trying to keep children safe.

Consider this, opportunities for measured risk-taking can create more able-bodied and self-assured children who will be better equipped to live safer lives in the long run than if we overly protect them to be safe in the momentary short term. If we stop children from being able to come in contact with perceived risky situations or elements in their worlds, we are setting them up to be less able to know how to be safe in the future when we are not around to protect them. We want durable, resilient, sensible children who grow up to become durable, resilient, sensible adults. If we jump in at every sign of danger, or have the goal of eliminating every chance of a hurt, loss, or injury, we are doing the development of that child an injustice. We are cutting out perhaps the most important aspect of growing up healthy and safe: coming in contact with risk, assessing it, and making one's own decisions about how to proceed, how to be safe. This can only truly come from experience and knowing who you are and what you can handle; and what you don't want to handle and would rather say "no" to. This is the very definition of an empowered and self-aware child.

This depth of self-knowledge and self-trust is the birthright of all children. We think we are protecting children by eliminating risk, but in doing so we may be contributing to far greater dangers in the long run.

Risk vs. Hazard

The old way of thinking about risk was to try to eliminate it. Manage it. Risk was bad. A four-letter word. It was something to be avoided, averted, reduced and removed. Especially when it came to children's environments. Licensing, liability, lawsuits. Insurance, inspectors, protectors. The push was to get rid of everything that could cause any kind of injury to anyone. Old sayings were "safety first" and "as safe as possible." Rules were established and regulations put in place. Now, that's not all bad, mind you. Some common sense changes to playground equipment designs were certainly necessary and have prevented many serious injuries over the years. Exposed concrete footings, battering ram swings, and protruding bolts and hardware are all good things to get rid of.

Here is where we need to establish a very important distinction: the difference between a risk and a hazard. In short, risks are good, hazards are bad. Risks are situations that a child can perceive and choose whether or not they want to participate. This could be balancing on a log, jumping off a rock, wrestling with a friend, or stepping in mud. These situations absolutely have a place in children's lives. As I'll keep repeating, risks in life are natural, necessary, and healthy to engage with.

A hazard, on the other hand, is something that is truly dangerous for a child: situations or objects that the child does not see, cannot make a logical choice about, and that have a definite chance of hurting them. The exposed concrete footing on the playground falls in this category. A child running or falling wouldn't necessarily expect a rough, unforgiving object to be in their path of play. Ouch. The same goes for broken glass, exposed rebar sticking out of the ground, a rabid woodchuck, a cliff, cars in the road, dead branches in a climbing tree, a rock under a climbing equipment buried under mulch. You get the idea. No fooling around: these sorts of things have absolutely no place in a child's environment and it is our job to be completely vigilant when it comes to removing all hazards from children's spaces. This is what daily playground inspections are all about. These are what playground safety guidelines are protecting children from.

And yet somewhere along the line risks and hazards were mixed up into meaning the same thing.

We now know that access to risk is beneficial to children's health and well-being. Risk is good. Risk is a positive thing. Risk is a natural part of life. In fact, learning to assess risk and deciding if you want to take a risk are essential skills for living. We all need to learn this and the best time to learn it is in childhood when everything is new and opportunities for growth are everywhere.

Get this: a child taking a risk balancing on a fallen log is learning a skill to be a better reader. Huh? Think about it: a preschool child sees a log on the ground. The child knows they could walk on it, but they could also fall off of it. They assess the situation. They decide if they want to attempt it. They decide to give it a go. They fall off! They get back on and try again. They try a new technique and inch along, inch along, inch along, and make it across. Success! They do it a few more times, feeling in their heart that deep sense of attempting something new, working for it, maybe failing a couple times, but then succeeding. Fast forward a few years to first grade with a book in their hand trying to sound out words. Learning to read those strange symbols is taking a risk and trying something that you've never done before. It takes courage and a belief that you can give it a go, maybe fail or fall, but keep trying and succeed. If you have past experiences of doing that, say, attempting to balance on a log as a preschooler and succeeding, you have that memory and self-knowledge that gives you confidence that you can take a risk, try something new, and ultimately succeed. *"I can do this. I'm going to read."* And each attempt and success gives the child a stronger sense of self-empowerment to tackle other life challenges. Practicing

a new sport is a risk. Making a new friend is a risk. Trying out for a play is a risk. Asking someone out on a date, driving a car, going to college, getting married are all risky endeavors that take a belief in oneself and confidence in one's resiliency to get through challenging situations. If we remove those opportunities from children's lives, we remove a key building block to the strength of one's character.

Another important component for the child is learning their *limits* for risk, knowing what they are and are not comfortable trying. We want children who can come across a risk, assess the situation, and firmly say "No. I don't want to do this." That skill comes from being able to judge for oneself and know oneself. Knowing when to walk away from a risk is just as important as knowing when to give a risk a shot. If we adults remove all risk or if we make the decisions for children about whether or not to try a risk we do children a great disservice—and have the potential to do them great harm. If we want children to be strong and thrive they need access to reasonable risks in their lives and have the freedom to make their own choices. What better place for them to do it than with you close by?

Risky Play

Another piece of the puzzle is that children *enjoy* play that is inherently risky. It's exciting, fun, daring. Children are growing and developing in every moment. They are constantly pushing the limits of what they have done before. It is what they are supposed to do. This is what childhood is all about—growing from infant to toddler, to preschooler, to the skills of a school-ager, to a teen to an adult. Each stage is a step past where the child was before. They are constantly moving beyond what they could do when they were smaller. They can only do this by pushing their limits, little by little. Now, they won't tell you they are striving for new developmental achievements. They are simply on a constant trajectory of growth and change. A baby wants to crawl. A toddler wants to walk. You're not going to tell a young toddler to not try walking because they might fall, are you? Of course not! It might hurt you a little each time they plop on their bottom or take a face-plant. But it's all in the name of healthy growth. The same goes for higher developmental limit-pushing behavior. Climbing trees, jumping from swings, skateboarding, bike riding, boogie boarding. If you are an adult you may call these activities "risky play." If you are a child you may simply call this "play."

So what's the difference? To help put things in perspective many researchers and educators have studied what they call "risky play," but there is still debate over the term. Should we use the word risky? Does that turn people off?

Is it too related to the old way of thinking that risk is bad? Maybe, but many agree that the term helps define certain types of play behaviors that children crave and adults, if present, have to breathe deeply when they see it, or look the other way. There is a widely accepted definition of risky play by Norwegian researcher and professor of physical education Ellen Beate Hansen Sandseter: **"Risky play can be defined as a thrilling and exciting activity that involves a risk of physical injury, and play that provides opportunities for challenge, testing limits, exploring boundaries and learning about injury risk"**.[3]

In a study that systematically categorized the various kinds of risky play through interviews and observations of children and staff in Norwegian preschools, Sandseter identified six categories of risky play.[4]

Categories and Subcategories of Risky Play[5]

Categories	Risk	Sub-categories
1. Great heights	Danger of injury from falling	• Climbing • Jumping from still or flexible surfaces • Balancing on high objects • Hanging/swinging at great heights
2. High speed	Uncontrolled speed and pace that can lead to collision with something (or someone)	• Swinging at high speed • Sliding and sledding at high speed • Running uncontrollably at high speed • Bicycling at high speed • Skating and skiing at high speed
3. Dangerous tools	Can lead to injuries and wounds	• Cutting tools: Knives, saws, axes • Strangling tools: Ropes, etc.
4. Dangerous elements	Where children can fall into or from something	• Cliffs • Deep water or icy water • Fire pits
5. Rough-and-tumble	Where the children can harm each other	• Wrestling • Fencing with sticks, etc. • Play fighting
6. Disappear/get lost	Where the children can disappear from the supervision of adults, get lost alone	• Go exploring alone • Playing alone in unfamiliar environments

Since that initial study she has added two more categories: "Play with Impact" (such as toddlers enjoying running and crashing into something), and "Vicarious Risk Experience" (children watching other children taking risks).

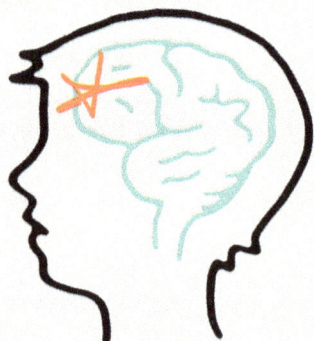

THE GOOD OL' PREFRONTAL CORTEX

Children love this stuff. And beyond that, science is showing that for healthy development they actually *need* it. Their brains crave it. **The prefrontal cortex** is the part of the brain that manages risk and controls emotion and do you know how it develops most fully and beneficially? **By being exposed to risk and emotion!** It needs those "on the edge" experiences to process the feelings and decision-making possibilities that go with a jump off a rock, or a splash in a puddle. This prefrontal cortex develops from childhood into early adulthood and it helps us learn how to handle risky behavior and to predict the consequences of our actions. It is wired to seek these risky experiences in order to make connections and learn. If we don't let children do it as youngsters climbing a tree, they'll be taking that part of their brain out for a spin behind the wheel of a car when they are teenagers. If adults step in to protect children from these kinds of activities as children, if we set the limits, how do they learn to set their own limits now or later in life? Without risky play as children they could lack tools to recognize their own limits. Their prefrontal cortexes could be sluggish as they work to imagine possible consequences of their actions. We may over-protect now and prevent some scrapes and bruises, but in the long run uncalculated risk-taking by young adults can get dangerous. Excessive adolescent risk-taking is not the only danger of over-protection by adults. There is also the new trend of excessive timidity in teens and young adults. Concerned teachers, principals, and college professors report that a generation of students are having great troubles dealing with small set backs and challenging situations—including normal "day in the life" experiences of any young adult. What used to be opportunities for students to grit their teeth, work harder, overcome obstacles, and strive for success are more and more frequently leading to emotional breakdown and giving up. Overprotected children can grow up feeling disempowered. When adults have managed children's risk their whole lives they can grow up unable to manage risk by themselves. They can get overwhelmed. They can have trouble making decisions. And since life is full of risk and uncertainty it can become, for the overprotected child, a life of stress and difficulty.

F.E.A.R.

But aren't we supposed to prevent children from getting hurt? Isn't that part of our job as adults? Don't they need us to keep them safe? Yes, and no. As with so much in life it is all about balance. It's about knowing the difference between times we truly need to step in from times we don't. **In truth, most of the time children don't need us to step in.** Just as we have built-in instincts to protect children, they have built-in instincts to protect themselves. We all do!

It's natural for us to worry. It's natural for us to protect. It's natural for us to see the dangers brewing when a child hops up on a log, or runs at a high speed, or picks up a large stick, or starts eating sand. We're wired to protect our young. It's an evolutionary trait that is built-in for the survival of our species. *Is that rustling in the bush a tiger? Is that snake poisonous? Are the children too close to that hot lava?!* It's built-in. Reflexive. And thank goodness. Here we are today thanks to generations of adults watching out for the dangers lurking in the shadows.

But…yet…and…we've somehow taken it too far in our day and age. **We've gotten too creative in our fear-based thinking.** I've got to hand it to us: we can see terrible things happening to children all the time everywhere. We're really good at that. "You'll poke your eye out!" "You'll break your neck!" Those fears of yesteryear seem almost quaint compared to what some adults can imagine happening to children today. Some of the blame rests on media—professional creative writers give it their best shot at creating horrifying, riveting television, movies, and online content. 24 hour news programming bombards us with situations that are extremely rare (that's why they are "newsworthy") but replay the events so much they seem commonplace to our tender hearts and minds. The combination of our internal wiring to protect our young, plus the media programming of our minds to think everything is unsafe, leads to an almost competitive situation among adults to be able to foresee the worst thing that could happen and to step in to stop it.

And if you don't think of these horrible things and

intervene before they happen, then there is also the fear that you might be judged by other adults as a negligent teacher/parent/caregiver. Couple all that with fears of liability if anything goes wrong under our watch and it can lead to adults filled with anxiety, stress, and fear. And because that feels so understandably uncomfortable it has lead us to severely limit children's opportunities for play. Yikes!

So what is a caring parent or adult working with children in the modern world to do? First step: take a deep breath. It's probably not that bad. In fact, most of this is only as bad as we make it. Only as bad as we believe.

The letters of the word itself can help us understand what it is all about:

F.E.A.R. — False Expectations Appearing Real

Fear-based thinking, while instinctual, can be overcome with mindfulness. Fear-based thinking occurs in our guts and brains. It's imaginative. When we see a child balance on a log our minds (our own prefrontal cortexes!) make up a scenario of what might happen. "Worst first" thinking predicts a fall with sustained injuries, perhaps even death! Our hearts race. We see it all play out. We need to do something right away. The mind imagines a frightening reality inside our heads, which compels us to take action in actual reality: "Get down from there Jimmy!" "Be careful Jimmy!" "No Jimmy, no!"

What if we were able to turn it around, use that creativity for good? Instead of seeing the "worst-first" in risky play situations, what if we saw the "best-first"?

Take two: What if as we see Jimmy hop on the log we instead let our prefrontal cortex flood with "best-first" imaginings such as Jimmy successfully balancing, smiling, moving along the log and jumping off with a heart full of pride and accomplishment? Notice your heart rate, your breathing. "He can do it" you think to yourself. Imagine how much better you might feel.

Now take three: instead of imagining anything happening to Jimmy, good or bad—since imagining is just making something up in our heads—we do something else: we just watch Jimmy. With an open heart and mind we watch the actual action going on without prejudgement, and determine the need for adult intervention, if any, based on the reality of what is truly happening, out there, in the world, outside of our heads. So simple! And yet it can be so hard. You're fighting against instinct to reverse a gut-reaction to protect at all costs.

©LoloStock / Adobe Stock

And yet, when we do, beautiful opportunities for children's play emerge. Play can actually play out. Jimmy can have his moment on the log. Jeannette can jump in the mud. Julian can curl up on the ground like a pill bug. Can you think of a time when you saw some risky play brewing and instead of jumping in you took a few moments to watch and see what happened? Well, what happened? Can you remember a time when you felt the urge to jump in and stop the play and you did stop it? What happened then? Or more importantly, what didn't get to happen?

This stuff is not easy to look at and it's not easy to change...or is it?

Finding Your Yes

This book is filled with amazing examples of children doing all sorts of kinds of play. Some of the play is quiet and sneaky, some wild and loud, some risky and edgy. There is a whole range of different kinds of kids doing different kinds of play. The one common denominator is an adult behind the scenes who said "yes." Children want to play, they want to be unleashed, but they are only allowed to do it when adults don't jump in and say no. The adults in this book have found their ways to say yes. Maybe you would feel comfortable saying yes in the same situations, but maybe you wouldn't. That's ok.

This book is about you finding *your* yes.

Finding out the kinds of play you are comfortable saying yes to. Finding out the kinds of play your school or program can feel comfortable with. There are certain situations we can all agree are too dangerous for children to be around (sharp rocks, cliffs, actual shark infested waters) but after that there is a wide spectrum among adults as to what is ok and what is not. Your yes is based on your history and your childhood experiences. Your yes is also based on the feelings and comfort levels of other adults you may be around. Those folks may have different thresholds for risk than you and that can have a big impact. Your yes is based on the philosophies and policies of the school or program you may work for. What is the culture of play? What are the core values and mission of the place? Does it support play or restrict play? Your yes is based on your children and their ability to navigate risk, get along with others, and assess their own comfort level with risky play.

Your yes is also based on knowing that you are not alone in wanting children to have more opportunities for the deep play experiences they crave. Knowing that children can be trusted to know their own limits. Seeing that it can be done and is being done. That others are finding their yes. That things are changing. And that you can change too.

And change does not have to happen in big ways overnight. Little by little is a-ok. **In fact, small steps are the best way to get going. "Dream big, Start small, Never stop" is the perfect motto for allowing more play to happen in your environment.** Deciding to change and getting people on board could be the trickiest part so make the first steps easy, small, barely noticeable. You don't need to give kids saws, hammers and nails to get the play going. Try putting out a cardboard box or two and stepping back to see what happens. Let the play go a teeny bit further than you might have previously. Watch what happens. Make mental notes. Add more loose parts. Observe the play.

The experience of saying yes may be surprising for children at first too. You might see them asking themselves, is it really ok? Is it not? You might need to reassure them that their play is ok. Maybe you talk with them about it first if that makes sense or helps you feel comfortable. Maybe you ask them to come up with ground rules they can all agree on. Once you do, once they get the smile and nod or the thumbs up from you they'll dive in deep and plunge into play. They are ready and willing to jump in, just waiting for cues from the adults. Or maybe you don't give any cues and just let it happen as an experiment.

The amazing thing is that once you cross the subtle line of allowing a little more risky play and see that everyone is ok, it becomes easier to do it again. As the children get used to the loosening of restrictions it becomes easier for them too. Pressure lifts and they are able to step up and regulate their play on their own. They can assess situations and decide what they want to do or not. Instead of them half-regulating their play and half trying to read your mind about what you are going to say about their play, the children are freed to be in the moment. Which makes them more present. Which makes them more aware. Which makes them more safe. And the more you do it and see it succeed, the less you have to hold your breath. The more you may be able to enjoy the play. The more you see how well the children are doing and how awesome and creative the play can become. Your job may have just become more fun!

At the same time you have to be more vigilant and watchful than you were before. To do all this successfully you really have to be on your game. No sleeping on the job here. You're taking it to the next level. It's far easier for adults to say "no." That's one reason so many caregivers say that word so often. You see some edgy play, you feel uncomfortable, you say no, stop it, and it's over. Done. Next! But, that's the old way of doing things and we've already discussed the ill effects that over "no-ing" can cause. So we know we want to find ways to say yes more, and when we do new kinds of play can emerge.

It doesn't mean we'll stop feeling uncomfortable! That's an important point. As we're on our guard, as we're allowing children to take more risks, we might end up feeling more uncomfortable than before. It's true. And really, when adults start feeling uncomfortable that's when they step in and stop play, even if the children are really fine. We'll do whatever we can to stop those uncomfortable

feelings. But with the tools and examples in this book, and your own trying this out little by little, **the hope is that you will learn to become more comfortable feeling uncomfortable.**

Let's be honest, you may never feel completely comfortable seeing a child climb in a tree, or sit in a mud puddle—and maybe you shouldn't—but when we have logged enough moments of seeing risky situations play out fine, the more we'll know that children can be ok. They can handle things. They can do it. We still may need to step in from time to time. We may still need to say no to things. But, we will have exercised our "yes" muscle and seen enough positive results that we will begin to develop a deep down knowing that things will most likely be ok. Most likely! But that's a big step from worst likely thinking. That ingrained, hard-wired, nervous protector voice is still there inside us. It still may be saying *"Are you crazy? Ohmigosh look what is happening! You better stop this! Quick!"* But because you have tried out stepping back instead of forward and you've seen the positive results you will hear a new voice inside that can add to the conversation. *"Now, now, let's watch for a moment. Take a breath. Let's see what happens. Susie has done this kind of thing before. She's pretty athletic and seems confident. I feel ok about this. We're right here if she needs us."* And suddenly, things do get a little easier for us. We still may feel that uncomfortable feeling pop up, we still have to sit with that, but we also know things can be ok. We know that we've actively done things to make ourselves feel better (as you'll learn in this book). We've confidently removed all hazards from the environment. We've analyzed risks and benefits of various play elements and activities. We've spoken to children about risky play. We've exercised our "yes" muscles with positive results and the positive messages keep getting stronger. When the uncomfortable feeling pops up we can acknowledge its presence, thank it for its concern, admire its creativity, and then reassure it the best we can. *"Things are going to be ok. Let's watch and be amazed."*

PHOTO BY KISHA REID

Licensor Censor

If you are at a school or childcare center what about the negative thought, *"licensing would never let us do that."* Dum-dum dum dum! Licensing is the Big Kahuna of negative thoughts that can stop us in our tracks from trying, or even thinking about trying exciting new play stuff with our children. You may see pictures in this book that might make you think, *"licensing would never let us do that," "licensing would say no,"* or *"licensing would have a cow!"* But remember now, we're adopting a mindset of *"yes."* Practicing what I'm preaching. Deep breaths. So let me say a little bit about licensing and perhaps more importantly: the *fear* of licensing…

F.E.A.R. OF LICENSING

We've all heard stories of tough licensors putting the kibosh on caregivers' well-intentioned ideas for the playground. Maybe that happened to you. Maybe that always happens to you! Or maybe not. But the fact is, licensors' thoughts and feelings about your program and environments are very important. Their perspective definitely matters. The good thing is that deep down we have the same goals and intentions: we all want children to have safe, happy childhoods and not get seriously injured along the way. **While every rule or regulation might not make absolute sense, they are all geared to the same end: healthy happy children.** Sometimes licensors interpret those rules differently than we might, and sometimes they get it wrong. And sometimes we get it wrong. I've heard more than one story of a center having a brilliant idea, fundraising, getting volunteers to build it, the kids playing on it and loving it, only to find out after the fact that it doesn't pass muster with the guidelines and, devastatingly, needs to get removed or seriously altered. That hurts. That's a bummer. And that could certainly color your feelings toward licensing and make you think twice about trying something special in the future.

I've also heard stories of licensors with the "old way of thinking" about risk, seeing hazards in silly things (like spoons in the sand pit) and making a center get rid of them. OK then. That's kind of tough and perhaps there needs to be some re-education and compassionate conversations with that particular licensor (or maybe with their supervisor). It's enough to turn you off and give you a mindset about what you can and can't be permitted to do in your playground or classroom. Totally understandable. But it's also dangerous because not only is it giving up your power to that licensor, you may start to give up your power to the *idea* of the licensor and what they might say. The *fear* of licensing can be a far worse danger and block to children's play and development than actual licensors and their work. It's true! As we know, fear is a "**F**alse **E**xpectation **A**ppearing **R**eal" and it can stop us in our tracks, keep us from considering our options, and even keep us closed to the possibilities that a book of ideas (like this) could offer. **Fear can stop good things from happening!**

So let's turn it around. Our book mantra is "yes" after all. Let's work on this as an example of how to turn a fear of licensing into an opportunity to say yes …

It's important to work with your licensor and regulatory people to create safe environments for your children that meet the rules and requirements for your situation. But do you know who you don't have to work with? The licensor in your head! So often when the fear of licensing pops up it stops the conversation before it even gets started. The fear of licensors seems to want to stop your creativity. (Whereas an actual licensor doesn't, believe it or not.) Don't you be more restrictive than your licensor! Don't censor yourself and your great ideas.

You can treat that voice just like that overprotective worrier in your head: *"I hear you. Thanks for thinking about this issue. But I have some ideas and strategies of my own that I think will make our ideas work."*

I know what you may be thinking, *"come on dude, get with the real world. Licensing is a fact of life. Get used to it. Our licensor is brutal. Nothing we can do."* Maybe, but maybe not. Let's consider some ways to work with our ideas and work with our real-world licensors. Let's let those knee-jerk censoring thoughts actually deepen the conversation instead of stopping it. Let them start the conversation and then work from there to creatively brainstorm how an idea may be realized to meet all the regulations and the licensor greeting it with enthusiasm. It can be done!

For over twenty five years, I've been working with schools and childcare centers to create natural playscapes in their outdoor environments. Together we've put in boulders, water features, mini-mountains, climbing walls, loose logs, hill slides, sand pits, mud digging areas and more. Sometimes the ideas would raise the eyebrow of the licensors, sometimes they wouldn't. One important thing I learned is that licensors want you to be doing the best work you can do. They want creative great things for children's environments, and they even have a sense of pride when the centers they work with do great things.

I also learned that, depending on your relationship with your licensor, the best time to bring them onto a playscape redesign project is… the very beginning. Then you can explain to them your concepts, philosophies, reasons and enthusiasm for doing what you are doing as well as the changes you want to make. That will help them understand the full picture and in turn can help them feel a part of the team to realize the dreams and help you on your way. A big way they can help is by identifying design features that have the potential to be sticking points with your regulations. (That kind of guidance is always better at the beginning than at the end.) Together you put your thinking caps on and adjust your design to pass the guidelines.

In my thinking that's how you "get around" licensing. You make your idea fit and work with the requirements. You do what you have to do to get at your real goal: the play objective that you want for your children. And that could be water play, digging, jumping off something high, mud, spoons!, anything. The thing to remember is, those goals can be accomplished in multiple ways: totally risky ways, perceived risky ways, barely risky ways, or no-danger-at-all ways. Don't be hung up on *one solution*. Be hung up on supporting the play possibilities and then *be flexible* on how you accomplish that goal. (That's sort of what we want children to be able to do too isn't it?) Can a mud kitchen be a mud kitchen without mud? Yes! Sand, dirt, gravel will do. Even just leaves and grass. Can a water play area be a water play area with no water? Well, not exactly, but a water play area can easily be made to follow health and safety guidelines such as not having standing water, or using clean fresh water at all times, or keeping it to a minimal trickle, or a bucketful that you as a caregiver fill up yourself. Even a "dry" river bed can be loads of fun.

The goals for your play space are more important than the exact way you manifest and reach those goals. The goals are the play possibilities: digging, building, hiding, climbing, jumping, balancing, etc. These have all been done thousands of different ways. People are doing it right now. Part of the beauty of children's imaginations in play is that anything can be anything. They don't need an authentic rocket ship to feel like they are in a rocket. Or a real deadly snake, or real hot lava. That's part of why cardboard boxes do so nicely in play. They can be anything at all. The most important thing is that you don't let anything stop you from providing the opportunities that you know children deserve. **Be clear with your focus and commitment to that goal then be flexible in how you work out the details so it can successfully manifest.**

Be flexible. Make it easy on yourself. Let the children play.

Check out licensing perspectives on page 178-181.

This Book + You

We're in it together. We're all working on balancing risk and safety and play. We all have our own yes's and we all have our own no's. We all have our own comfort levels when it comes to risky play and we have our internal struggles. But we also have our own dreams for our children. We want them to thrive and be healthy, happy, and safe in the long run and in the now. We know that things have gotten a little wacky with fear, safety, and overprotectedness. We know that adults have tended to over-correct when things go wrong or when folks are fearful of things going wrong.

Now it's time to re-correct and redirect our work with children. The stakes are too high to let things keep going on autopilot. It's time to take back the controls!

How do we do that? This book is designed to help. It may provoke you, it may startle you, it may make you throw the book down and run away. But hopefully it will also excite you, empower you, and inspire you. You'll see pictures of children doing all sorts of amazing things. Sometimes edgy, sometimes risky, but always authentic, always real.

What you may not see as much in the pictures are the adults who are allowing the play to happen. For good reason we see children as the heroes of their play. But adults are heroes too, because they have found ways to allow play to happen, say yes, to support the play, to facilitate the play, to observe the play diligently if necessary. There they are, living their principles in their practice. And here we are, timidly or excitedly ready to take things to the next level. The book in your hands is here to help.

There are so many exciting things happening in this movement to restore children's play. All-outdoor "forest schools" are popping up in huge numbers around the world. Elementary schools are reinstating and reimagining recess for students with less rules and more loose parts and choices for play. Childcare centers are creating mini "anarchy zones" where children can build and create with loose parts, mud and mess. Parent and school groups are coming together for free play sessions in parks, natural settings, and backyards. Whole cities are working to become more playful and child-friendly to support children's free play. International Mud Day is a beloved and much-celebrated worldwide phenomenon. (You know about International Mud Day of course, right??) The well-established European profession of "playwork" is spreading around the world inspiring us with tools and tips to support more free play. Non-profit groups, government organizations, and businesses are pledging to work together to support children's free play with play charters, play policies, and collective writing of national risk-benefit assessment frameworks to support risky play. And people like you are working with children everyday to allow children to make their own choices about their play. It all feels like a breath of fresh air and a relief. It's long overdue, and yet right on time.

Together, we can make this change.

So fasten your seat belts, I've got lots to show you in this book! Things will get wild and messy but we'll start slowly with concepts to make you rethink your role as play supporter and tools the "pros" use to feel more comfortable with riskier play. Then you'll be ready to progress to flipping the world back right-side-up with an in-depth look at activities children absolutely need to be doing but that somewhere along the line adults deemed too risky and eliminated. (Mud. Fire. Chickens!) I'll lobby for their re-inclusion in the lives of children and we'll see how lots of groups have stood up to pressure and found ways to incorporate this stuff in children's environments. Then it's pictorial tour time of "best practice" examples from around the world of this kind of right-side-up thinking including: childcare centers, elementary schools, forest schools, and adventure playgrounds. And by then I know you'll be fired up and ready to give it a go in your own play worlds so let's do this!

PART 2

Ways to Support Risky Play

Childhood

If you want to have more risk in your children's space what's the one thing you can add to ensure it? Children! That's right. Children are natural daredevils and explorers who want to "go for it" and push the limits. You know it's true. Your nerves may be shot and your hair may be turning grey but you love it. Maybe you are a Zen master and can breathe your way through the wild ways of children. Or maybe you stand firm in your limits of rambunctious play. Maybe you have a soft spot for the intricacies of play because you still have a connection to the child you once were and the play that was important to your life growing up. **What do you remember?**

I think the best place to start this book-journey is remembering. Who were you as a child? What did you like doing? Where were some of your favorite places to play? Did your mother or father know what you were doing there?? Were you "free range" or were you watched-over or "helicoptored?" **Every family is different. Every generation is different. Do you remember taking any risks as a child? Do you remember saying no to risks?**

I remember a gigantic rope swing in the woods that swung out over a packed dirt ravine with a little creek at the bottom in a nearby neighborhood. Friends brought me there and invited me to swing. It gave me pause. Sure, *they* did it all the time. The big kids were confident enough to do acrobatics across as they swung and younger kids also happily hopped on the knotted rope and zoomed off over the abyss. But I wasn't so sure. Not *everyone* did it. Some kids were happy to just poke around the bushes and wander along the bank. It definitely wasn't for everybody.

Was it for me? I wish I could tell you that I grabbed that fat rope, took a deep breath, and pushed off over the void with a beating heart and an exhilarated self-esteem. But to tell you the truth that's not the part that sticks with me. **It's the *edge* that I remember most. That line between should I or shouldn't I? Can I do this? Can I not do this? Do I even *want* to do this? Yes? Or no?** There were no adults there making up my mind for me, telling me what I should or shouldn't do. It was up to me to decide. I was responsible for my own well-being. My own safety. My own success.

Did that experience help make me a teenager and adult who was able to handle stress and risk in a healthy way? Maybe. Who knows? What I do know and can vividly recall as a child was a deep, knowing voice inside that was there to help me make decisions about my safety.

We all have that voice inside. We tap it both for our own well-being and for our children when we worry about their safety. It's our very own built-in red alert system. It's important to remember that children have that system too. And their inner knowing gets stronger and clearer with the more risks they are able to confront. Their yes's get stronger and their no's get stronger too. Allowing the child to make their own decisions about risk is what's vitally important. Yes, it's our job to keep them safe. But more importantly, it's our job to let *them* learn how to keep themselves safe.

You learned as a child, right?

Relationships with Your Children

It's all about relationships with your children. You know your kids. You've seen them through a lot. A parent or caregiver is there to witness the whole world of childhood happenings, seeing children grow and learn on a daily basis. One thing that makes play in a public park different than play at recess or a childcare center is that the adults are there with the children day after day. They know what's up. They know what to expect. They know what to look out for. You know who has great balance and coordination and who doesn't. You know who is fearless. You know who is timid. You know who pushes the limits too much and should have a little more fear. And you know who is thoughtful in their risk-taking. That's the beauty of extended time with children. You get to know them in a deep way. It also lets you provide a rich learning environment filled with a variety of elements for a variety of children. Some kids need a giant boulder to jump from. Others don't. Some children need hand-holding. Others don't. Plus everybody is changing and growing all the time. It keeps you on your toes! And yet because you know your children so well you are in the best position to make decisions about their risk-taking activities.

Authorities coming into your yard for the first time may not immediately understand what is going on. New parents touring the school might gasp in fear. Other parents may shake their heads in disbelief. But they don't know what goes on in the yard like you do. Rain or shine, grouchy or joyous, your children are out there doing their thing. You and the children have history. And that informs every opportunity and item that you provide for the children. That's what you have that licensors coming cold into your yard don't have and that is part of what you need to be able to show them when they have questions about what's going on. They need to see the history. A good licensor can imagine it, sense it and see the faded memories of children climbing fallen logs and succeeding. Or a child falling and deciding to wait for a while and before trying again in a week or two. You have the knowledge. You base your decisions on your relationships. You have discussions with children about it all. You answer children's questions about risky things. You challenge them to do thinking on their own. All this goes on every day and it informs the decisions you make about risk and the things you allow to happen. Not all children can handle everything. You know what your children can handle and how to best support them.

Ways to Support Risky Play 35

For example: to the left is a picture of my son JJ and his friend Zara on a rickety-looking but sturdy thing we built at a spring spruce-up build day a few years ago at their preschool. The project had nearly zero budget so we built with scavenged pallets. Don't worry, I built it solid. I started my career working as a designer for a playground equipment manufacturer and all that stuff is governed by strict rules and regulations to protect children's safety. I've been trained as a playground safety inspector and always work to make things safe and sturdy. However, I was showing this image and talking about safety to a group of educators in Montana a few years ago when participants called me out saying, "Safety?! Come on Keeler, there's a saw on the ground under them. And a brick! And no safety surfacing." You might be thinking the same thing. And I admit that on seeing this image cold, with *no context* it might seem like a hazardous accident waiting to happen.

But here's the thing: I know these two kids. They know me. I've seen them climbing and jumping and falling and laughing and crying since they were babies. They know their way around an elevated wooden platform let me tell you, and are perfectly fine managing themselves around something like this. You can't tell that from a picture and you couldn't tell that if you had just suddenly arrived on the scene. But me, I didn't think anything of them being up on top. I was proud of my pallet contraption and happy they were attracted to it to climb, dance and jump off and I wanted to get some pictures. True, if this was a typical day at the daycare we'd certainly make sure there was no sharp saw underneath for heaven's sake, no loose brick, and no bags of hardware. But it was a special day and in truth Zara and JJ helped me hammer and saw this thing together. They were aware there was a saw on the ground. They might have been the ones who left it there!

Only you can explain the history you have with your children. Only you can make sense of it. How do you say *"I know these kids will be all right"* to someone seeing it cold? How can you convince someone else that you know what you are doing when your work is so intuitive and subjective?

The first step could be looking within and analyzing the reasons you are permitting a risky activity. In my case I may remember times when JJ and Zara were in my yard on that *other* scrap wood play thing we built with found materials. "*Yes, they climbed that thing and were fine. They sat up on top, played with cars on it, and jumped off. True,*

I remember Zara running into one of the "walk the plank" boards we had sticking off the top. But I also remember we set up a board blockade on the fly to keep that from happening again. Both kids have taken gymnastics classes and are pretty well coordinated. Both kids dance and boogie. Both kids love each other…but, I've also seen them each push each other so I'll keep an eye on that. So far they just look like they are having fun and getting along, so no worries yet."

All that could have been going in my mind consciously or subconsciously as they climbed up and started dancing

and jumping. To the outsider it may look like I am not concerned about their safety. To some people it might even look like I'm not paying attention because I'm not panicking and saying *"Be careful! Be careful!"* (Have you noticed that panic is contagious?)

Now, if a child that I didn't know very well climbed up on top I would have had a very different feeling about it. Giving the child the benefit of the doubt I might have watched first before saying anything, but I would also keep a much closer view of them and even perhaps move to be in range of catching their fall if need be.

I can assure you that if I turned around and saw that a *toddler* had found their way on top of that pallet palace I would step in as quickly (and calmly) as possible and remove them. (You really do need to watch toddlers. They'll try anything!)

Nobody knows your children and the dynamics of your backyard or grounds the way you do. It takes a lot of internal processing to make sure things go smoothly and it will never look the same way to an outsider. But don't let that stop you from letting your children do what you know they are capable of doing!

Trusting Children

Pippi Longstocking—rebel, renegade, independent thinker. This literary hero is an icon of the self-assured, creative child. Besides the fact that she is the strongest girl in the world, part of the fun and appeal of Pippi's story is that she, unlike her neighbor friends and other kids she meets, is not subject to the whims, fears or agendas of adults. She lives on her own—with her pet monkey and horse—and quite likes it that way, thank you very much. No adult is going to tell her what to do. And no adult need worry about her. She can handle herself quite nicely. Out on a walk with her friends she goofs around, falls in a ditch and gets soaking wet. She couldn't care less. Her friends are distraught, saying, *"but now you're soaking wet." "What's wrong with that?"* Pippi responds. Hmmm. **What *is* wrong with that? Why do things seem to bother us more than they bother children?**

Well, for one thing, it could mean more work for us! If a child gets muddy or wet at school or childcare it could be a big deal, depending on how well-equipped we are to handle it. Someone gets wet and suddenly we might have to deal with it, take the child inside, get them undressed and redressed. But wait, we need to keep our adult-kid ratio in line so now six other children have to come inside while one child gets changed?! And wait again, what if that child doesn't have extra clothes? Then what to do about the wet clothes? And then what will the parents say about all this?? Oy. It's easier to keep them dry. It's easier to keep them inside. What's wrong with kids getting wet? *"It makes my life more complicated!!"* And it does, if we're only geared up to have dry, clean children. If we only think that proper play involves no mess or wet clothes or rainy days or snow or mud.

Pippi Longstocking from the book by *Pippi Moves In* by Astrid Lindgren and Ingrid Vang Nyman[6]

If we believe that children actually need to experience it all, the good, bad and the messy, then it is our job to facilitate it happening. We switch our way of thinking from *"everything should be clean and tidy"* and *"if anything goes wrong it's an ordeal"* to: *"mud happens and wet happens, and messy clothes happen—and it's good."* It's all in the service of learning, fun and exploration and we shouldn't let adults' clean agendas stand in the way. Our job is not to keep children clean. Our job is to support their play and growth the best way we can. And if that means we have to have extra clothes on hand either from parents or garage sale hand-me-downs, so be it. If it means we need a make-shift changing station outside so be it. If it means we need to deal with wet, slimy clothes then we need to find a way to give service with a smile and know that this isn't something that we have to do *instead* of caring for our children, or guiding them or teaching them. This *is* the honored work of supporting children's play. Dealing with wet pants isn't beyond our job or beneath it. It is our job. We shouldn't think of it as *more* work for ourselves. It is simply *the* work. All in the service of loving and tending to the children in our care.

And children can be a part of the changing from wet to dry clothes and taking care of their extra clothes in ways that make your job easier. Bring them into it. Help them be helpers. **The spectacular moments of childhood magic often happen in the tiny times that have nothing to do with our adult wishes and preconceived ideas of what our jobs should be.** We are realizing that to support all kinds of play our jobs may involve putting new systems in place that deal with the messes of play.

So how can we learn to agree with children and say, *"what's wrong with that?"* Play is the goal, and allowing children to play with less interference from us is also a goal. Putting new methods and plans in place are the means to that end.

Trusting children to know their needs, cares, and limits is part of the picture as well. Here is a sequence from the grand sand and water play area of Kent State University's Child Development Center. It was cold and rainy the day I was visiting. We adults all had rain slickers and coats keeping us warm and dry. Some children did too. But not all of them. Some children had rain boots, but other children were barefoot! In the rain! On a cool day! Egads! Did it slow them down? Not a bit. If anyone got cold feet (literally) they could go in to warm up and put on socks and boots. I didn't see any children do that. Everybody was busy. They had important canal digging, river making, sand digging, and lake building to do! I saw engaged, excited, focused, collaborating children having a great time doing great work, having great play, and enjoying a rainy day. *"Rain, rain go away, come again some other day?"* More like *"rain, rain, what's wrong with that?"* Once again I was inspired and proud of the children for their beautiful energized play and… I was inspired and proud of the adults behind the scenes allowing it to happen. The first thing to cheer about here is that on a rainy day the adults even let them go out! Hooray! Nobody looked out the window and said, "it's raining, we can't go outside." They looked out and said "it's raining, grab what clothes you need to go out." I also loved that they let the children decide for themselves how wet they wanted to get. Some: not very wet so they wore hoods and coats and boots and rain pants. Others: semi-not wet with coats and boots. Others: sort of wet with coats but no boots. Others: soaked with no coats or boots or anything.

The adults here trusted children to know what they wanted to wear and how they wanted to play. The children weren't bothered and they weren't hesitating from having fun outside. Boots might get in the way of really feeling the sandy water flow, y'know! You could tell this place had a deep culture of play with systems in place to facilitate it. Indeed: rainy days made different kinds of work necessary for the adults: stripping wet clothes off children, putting clothes in washers and dryers, then putting clean dry clothes on children. But this school found ways to do it that worked for them. You could too. Yes, there are certainly more steps to going outside on wet days, but when we truly care about children's experiences of play and exploration…what's wrong with that?

Ways to Support Risky Play 43

PHOTO BY KISHA REID

Risk-Benefit Analysis

Ok, here it comes. This could be the most important subject of the entire book and the most important piece of the puzzle to help you find new ways to say yes! Risk. Benefit. Analysis. Instead of doing just a *risk* analysis of play and play yards, professional people the world over, now do *risk-benefit* analysis. There are benefits to all the risky stuff that must be be considered in the conversations we have about children's environments and play. Risk-benefit analysis is a tool that we can all use to help us determine what is an acceptable risk in our yards, and what is not acceptable. What is reasonable risk? What is unreasonable risk? Where do we draw the lines between our yes's and no's? Risk-benefit analysis is the tool to help us decide.

I first heard about risk-benefit analysis from the world of forest schools and nature kindergartens. These are the amazing schools you may have heard of where children are outside in the woods and nature all day long in all kinds of weather, all year long. (I'll get deeper into the philosophy and practice of these types of schools later in the book, complete with a tour of some inspirational forest school settings, but for now know that these are the places that let kids climb rocks and trees, jump in mud, cook over open fires, balance on logs, play with sticks.) It's not surprising that children thrive in these settings since this is the stuff that most children love doing when allowed to explore and play in nature. What first amazed me was that these children were allowed and supported to do this kind of play in licensed educational settings. Fire? Yes. Ice? Yes. Goats? Yes! In school? Yes!! How were those adults able to say yes to so many seemingly dangerous and risky things?

One of the tools of their trade… is the risk-benefit analysis. They know that a lot of these activities can be risky. They don't pretend that they are not. Instead, they carefully consider all the *risks* of a certain activity or element in a child's environment and write them down.

But they don't stop there!

Next they write up all the **benefits** of the same activity or element. They create an exhaustive list of both possibilities and then decide, "Do the possible benefits outweigh the possible risks? Or do the risks outweigh the benefits?" They also list the possible *interventions* and *management* that could be done to reduce the possibility of injuries. With deeper analysis they may also weigh in on the *likelihood* of the risks occurring as well as the actual *severity* of the possible injury to help them decide. Is the fall a potential for a scratch? Or a plunge into actual hot lava? All these ideas and considerations are brought together in discussions and debates with teachers and staff—and children too—until finally decisions and consensus can be reached.

Yes we can climb this fallen log. No we cannot scale this cliff. Yes we can scale this cliff but only this high. This works for the Norwegian children who want to ice fish in subfreezing weather and it can work for your own yard when children want spoons to dig in the sand.

The exercise starts as a tool to decide what activities to allow then becomes a lasting record of the adults' thinking and consideration of the risky elements. Some schools have their risk-benefit assessments stored in file cabinets in their offices. Others have them collected in three-ring binders and kept in classrooms, out-buildings or storage sheds. These write-ups can be used to show authorities the mindful thought process and steps taken to reduce injuries. They can also act as a training manual and guideline for new staff as they learn the philosophy and protocols of the new environment. The risk-benefit analysis is a key tool to help these forest-schooling adults find their yes and it can help you find your yes too.

DYNAMIC RISK-BENEFIT ANALYSIS

We want to say yes more, but children push the limits and we see danger. In split seconds we scan a situation and make decisions whether to allow play or stop play. Even as super-supporters of play we do that *and we should be doing that*. It is our job to make those decisions about our children's safety. But how do we make those decisions? What do we take into consideration? What inner guidance are we listening to?

If we analyze our thinking a little more deeply, we find that we are already actually doing on-the-fly dynamic risk-benefit analyses. We may see someone on a log and think, *"she's gonna fall and poke her eyes out!"* But on some level we are also scanning the situation and saying *"is she really going to fall and poke her eyes out?"* This all happens fast and sometimes we only give the danger-seeing part enough time to react. Things happen quickly with children and sometimes that's the only thing there is time for!

I can assure you that inside of us there is also another observing voice that is seeing and whispering the possible *benefits* of a certain activity. That voice can get overshadowed. It can get cut off. It can easily be ignored. But we can also learn to develop that voice and see more clearly what it sees. But it takes practice. A loud panicky voice about poking eyeballs taps that primal protector in us and that's fine. We need that voice. But we also need the calmer voice. The more thoughtful voice. The voice that sees the light in any situation. Like yin and yang we need to bring each voice into balance. Both voices are important to be able to best protect children from serious injury while living our ideals to support play the best way we can. Practice, practice, practice.

A great way to get some practice is by going through the risk-benefit analysis process on any given element your children might encounter. Imagine a child doing almost anything: sitting on a log, jumping from a log, holding a worm, eating a worm, carrying a stick, carrying a long branch, wading in water, picking raspberries, pushing a lawnmower, picking poison ivy, picking their nose, running, running with scissors! The list obviously is infinite. Even as you read those items you were probably doing mini dynamic risk-benefit analyses. As you thought of some of those activities your blood pressure remained calm. *"Sit on a log? Sure, no problem."* A vision of a sunny day with a child happily sitting on a log smiling with butterflies fluttering around may have popped into your head. The voice whispering benefits was easy to hear. A romantic scene with lots of positive possibilities.

Jumping from a log though? That might've gotten your attention more and perked the ears of your protector voice. That's a little more risky. Yes to some benefits but there could be danger too—how high is that log? What are they jumping into? Is there anything under the log that could hurt them? Are they good jumpers? Split second wonderings. Hold a worm: maybe. Eat a worm: come on, Keeler. Some things are easy to imagine the positives, others obviously not. Dynamic risk-benefit analysis takes practice and with limited time in the moment we may lean more one way than the other.

Taking time for deliberate risk-benefit analysis helps open things up for careful consideration.

So let's go through the process. Pick a topic, any topic. Here we can study having a log in the yard. You can do this exercise on your own first or follow along. Make a chart in a notebook: risks, benefits, management. There is a blank chart in the Extra Stuff section of this book. I'll walk you through it. Your analysis might be the activity of a child doing something on a log—jumping, balancing, etc. Or it might be a more basic analysis like simply having a log in the yard.

BENEFITS

You can pick risks first, you can pick benefits first, or you can go back and forth with your ideas. Let's pick benefits first. Picture your basic log. List all the benefits that children (and you) may get by having this log around. Here goes:

- It's nice having a natural material in your space
- Children get to touch wood
- You can sit on it
- You can roll it
- You can jump from it
- *...Can you think of anything else?*

Be creative! (you'll definitely get creative thinking about the risks)

And in this corner:

RISKS

OK, let your mind go. Picture all the bad stuff that could happen. Really go for it!

- Splinters!
- Sharp edges
- Wood can crack over time
- A child could fall off
- It could tip over
- *...Can you think of anything else?*

MANAGEMENT

This is a key factor to the process. This list describes all the things you could do to help minimize the chance of injury and of all that bad stuff from happening. The competition between risks and benefits could be neck and neck but if you manage the object or situation appropriately that could tip the balance to a place where you feel comfortable saying yes. It's best to discuss management in a group with all the adults involved. With kids too!

- Sand edges smooth
- Select wood that doesn't splinter
- Sand any cracks and splinters that develop
- Be on the lookout for bees
- Talk to children about how they think it should be best used safely
- *...Can you think of anything else?*

If you were doing this exercise on your own, maybe you'd write all the ideas on paper then review it. Perhaps you'd write it on a whiteboard in a staff meeting for a group discussion. Either way, now it's time to make some decisions.

Should you? Shouldn't you? The next step is to review the risk-benefit analysis (RBA) thoughts and weigh the differences. The million dollar questions: *do the risks outweigh the benefits? Or do the benefits outweigh the risks?* What do you think? (You may have different risks, benefits, and management ideas than I did in this example so take those into consideration instead of mine.)

Risk-Benefit Analysis for a Log

BENEFITS	RISKS
It's nice having a natural material in your space	Splinters!
Children get to touch wood	Sharp edges
You can sit on it	Wood can crack over time
You can roll it	A child could fall off
You can jump from it	It could tip over
You can build with it	A child could trip over it
Children can imagine it's something else: a robot, a dog, a building, a car, a friend	You could fall on it
You observe what happens to the log over time - it may change color, rot, disappear	It gets all rotted
It becomes a science experiment over time: what lives in a rotting log?	Worms and bugs!
Children can make wood chips from it	Logs disintegrate then you don't have them anymore
Carrying it is a good upper body workout	It could roll into someone
You can count the tree rings and talk about how old the tree was	It's loose and wobbly
You can study the bark	It's challenging to balance on (some play elements could be benefits and risks)
Builds positive self-esteem with successful jumps and balances	Stubs your toe
It can be challenging to balance on	Gets you dirty
It can be a small stage for performances	Gets wet in rain, slippery and slimy
It could be a small mud kitchen table	Might attract lumberjacks (?)
Rolling and balancing on it is a super coordination challenge!	Bees could make a nest inside
As it disappears over time it shows children that everything in life changes	Could poke your eye out

MANAGEMENT	
Sand edges smooth	Place it in a space away from fixed playground equipment
Select wood that doesn't splinter	Install it firmly in the ground
Sand any cracks and splinters that develop	Know where to dispose of rotten logs
Be on the lookout for bees	Know where to get replacement logs
Talk to children about how they think it should be best used safely	Have the ends roughed up with a chainsaw for better traction
	Inspect the log every morning during your playground safety inspection

My answer is Yes! (You probably expected that) but it doesn't stop there. The conversation keeps going: How many logs should we bring in? Should they be kept in a certain area? When should we talk to the children about the logs? How do we best implement all of our management strategies? ...And there you go. You are on your way. You've either considered the options and deemed it a no-go, or you've reviewed your process and given it the thumbs up, with work to do on your part.

This could all happen informally if the topic was easy (a log for example). You might just touch base with your fellow staff members and say "log?" And they'd think about it and say yea or nay. A decision could happen quickly. But the risk-benefit analysis process digs deeper and is especially important for the stickier topics, some of which we'll get to later in this book.

The process should give you the confidence in your "yes-ing" that you've considered the real possibilities. *And* the RBA becomes a formal document that you can show new staff, parents, licensors, insurers and anybody else who is curious about your thought-process. If an authority questions you on you having a log in your play area you can grab your thick three-ring binder, thunk it down on the table, and have an in-depth conversation about the process you went through to make your decision to say yes. You're not making these decisions haphazardly, the log didn't appear there without you knowing it, you understand the risks of having such a log. But you also understand the benefits and methodically made a decision to say yes. This type of thinking impressed me the first time I saw it and I believe it will impress those you show it to as well. It helps make the case for your philosophy and how you put it into practice. *"Wow, you really thought about this."* You care about children's safety, but you also trust your children and care about their freedom, exploration, and opportunities to learn about the world around them through direct experience. The RBA is a key tool to help you find your ways to say yes.

I might as well do a bit of lobbying for logs in the play space while we're on the subject. Ah logs, how do I love thee? Let me count the ways....So first of all anywhere that trees grow, trees also fall down, lose branches, and need to be trimmed or removed. There is a nearly endless supply of potential logs available to you because someone somewhere is always chopping down or chainsawing parts of a tree. All you need to do is connect with them, let them know you could use some logs for your play area and soon enough you'll have all the log chunks you want. Check in with your neighbors or parents of your students. If a tree blows down in your neighborhood don't be afraid to stalk the homeowner and ask if you can have some of the tree if they don't mind! Form a relationship with local tree service companies and your department of public works or city forester. They remove trees all the time and are usually delighted to chop some pieces up "for the kids."

Once you have the logs you can plant them solidly in the ground as a balance way or retaining wall or leave them loose for children to drag or roll around during their play. Here's a scene at a fun preschool where they have log chunks lining their sand pit. Children also use them as challenging hop-to-hop traverses. Should they be allowed? Shouldn't they? That's what you do your RBA for! Even if you say "sure, no problem" you are still doing dynamic RBA's depending on the day, the condition of the log, the muddiness, the skills of the child about to

Ways to Support Risky Play 51

embark on the adventure (let alone their current mood or blood sugar level). There are so many factors that go into you saying yes!

This group said yes to logs and here they are saying yes to the boy in red making his careful way across. The caregiver is just behind him sitting on a log (they make nice seats too y'know) and by his obvious level of comfort, concentration, and not appearing to be rebelling he knows it is ok for him to do this activity. Do you think he should be able to do this activity? It does look a little risky. But does he look like he can handle it? He does to me. I'd watch him and see how it goes (after scanning the ground for any hazards he might not see if he accidentally fell). So, step by careful step he goes from one log to another. He even raises the ante a bit by building a totally wobbly bridge from another loose chunk of wood. Whoa! He wobbles, but keeps himself upright. A younger child nervously watches from behind the teacher.
"Wow, look at him go. I'd like to try that…but it's risky. Will I make it across like the big guy? Will I fall?" The big guy continues, makes it each step of the way. The littler boy finally catches up only to see the bigger boy build another wobbly bridge to go across.

"Oh man, I made it this far but do I have to do that sketchy bridge too?"

No, of course you don't Jimmy. It's up to you…

52 Adventures in Risky Play

Playwork

What if I told you there was a highly-skilled, specialized profession solely and purely dedicated to providing the time, space, and materials for children's free play? These people are not teachers or childcare providers. They are not social workers or play therapists or coaches. They are *playworkers* and the profession is *playwork*. Born in the adventure playground movement after World War II in Europe and Japan, playwork has a long rich history of real-world practice and academic refinement with clearly established and agreed upon principles guiding their work.

Playworkers are tireless, vocal supporters of play provision and policy for cities and municipalities and they have a deeply thoughtful practice working "in the field" with children of all ages and abilities every day in a variety of scenarios and situations—schools, parks, playgrounds, neighborhoods, summer camps, "pop-up" play days, etc. They are the masters of supporting children with the lightest intervention possible, saying *yes absolutely* to children's play, and knowing that the best way to allow play to happen is to step back and watch it go. Playwork has informed a lot of my thinking about adults' roles with children and it can be an important guide for all of us as we work to say yes to play. Playworkers have been doing it for over 75 years and they have a lot to teach us!

A playworker may think of themselves as a *helper* for play. Not a leader, or an organizer or someone controlling play. Far from it. They want children free to do whatever they want so a playworker tries to stay out of the way. They may help set up a space by putting out materials children can use during play like boxes, boards, balls, tubes, fabric or paint. They may do a little modeling of play, stacking things here and there to give children a hint that it's ok to play like this or that. **But then they get out of the way.** Some children need more help with play so a playworker may be called in to do some heavy lifting, rolling a giant tire here, hoisting a big bucket of water. A playworker may know some good knots to help children in their ropey swing-building adventures. A playworker might be the keeper of the sharp tools and help cut holes in a cardboard box castle if asked. They may pick flowers to add to the mud kitchen for soups and concoctions. They may join in a pool noodle battle or a burdock seed ball war, as long as they don't mind getting repeatedly whacked or stuck with burdocks. We all have our personal boundaries.

Also noteworthy: playworkers may often look like they aren't doing anything. If you stumble upon an adventure playground staffed with playworkers or a childcare center with playwork-trained caregivers it might seem that the adults are being lazy. They aren't playing with the children. They might be just standing around. But look closer and you'll see what's going on: they're watching intently. They've got a careful eye on things. Their bodies might be still as they watch some wild play happenings but their eyes will be scanning and their heart may be beating quickly too. (As you know watching risky play can be nerve-wracking.) But like lifeguards at the pool these people are ready to dive in and save somebody if they need to. Just as we are practicing trusting children to know their own limits, playworkers trust them too and believe that most of the time children are fine on their own. **But not always!**

STEPPING BACK

Playworkers work hard to rein in the adult knee-jerk reaction to step in to stop risky play. They may position themselves to step in if necessary, but because they believe so deeply in children they've trained themselves to have a *new* knee-jerk reaction to risky play: instead of immediately stepping in they may first step back. And keep their mouths shut. They observe what's going on and do on-the-fly risk-benefit analyses of the situation to decide if these children can handle what's going on

and what potential risks might await them. I've done this playworking many times. *OK, this big guy is being creative. Rolling tires down a mulch mountain, watching how far they go. I'm making sure no little kids are walking in the path of the tires. Keeping the coast clear. Now the big kid is building a jump for the tire out of boards.*
Love it! Ok, no little kids around this time either. "Looking good!" And as the tire sails through the air, calling out "Nice!"

Or, the playworker may watch a child make a daring leap off a straw bale stack over and over. They are ready to act if necessary, but know the child is probably fine. *This guy looks pretty agile. He's got this. I'll stand between him and the tree, not to interfere but if he jumps too far he'll hit me and not the tree trunk. That's a good thing. He's holding a rope and jumping. Could be sketchy but the rope isn't actually doing anything. I don't need to say anything about the rope, certainly not "Be careful." Here he goes. Whoa! OK, good landing. Other children coming too. Are they staying out of the way? Yes, they look fine. No one wants to get hit. Up he steps to the top of the stack, rope in hand and ready….and down he goes! Head first! Is he ok? Feet pointing to the sky….and he's fine.*

ADULTERATING PLAY

The playworker's job is to be in service to the children and to the play. They might "stage" an area with materials for play before children arrive. They may give the thumbs up to the play children want to do. They may get asked to play by the children and happily join in the fun. Here again they don't want total control; their participation is not about the adult and how Peter Pan-ish and playful they can be. It's about the children and supporting the play that spirals and flows from moment to moment. If the playworker can help support or prolong the play, great. If it sputters out on its own, that's fine too. Sometimes playful adults have a hard time not being in charge or not feeling like a Pied Piper leading the children and play. Playworkers work hard to resist that temptation too. Playworkers try not to *adulterate* the children's play. That is, they don't mess with it. They don't try to change the play, they don't narrate the play, and they don't look for "teachable moments." Their only adult agenda is to support the play. Adulterating play alters the play and can wreck it. Is the play about the children or is it about us? It's about the children.

SELF-REFLECTIVE PRACTICE

The deeper you go with this whole supporting children's play idea, the trickier it gets. That's why another key aspect of a playworker's job is *self-reflective practice*. Every day they think about the job they did with their children. They reflect on what they think went right, and what didn't go so well. They talk with their co-workers about the jobs they did. It's not always easy to admit when you didn't live up to your ideals. Or when you think you messed up. But that's how you get better. That's how you can support more play in the future. You also get to celebrate what went right and feel what it feels like to help play. Some playworker groups take time to journal at the end of the day about the experiences and how the playwork went. Other groups take time to talk it out with fellow staff. Sometimes you only have time to think about it after work on your way home. Either way, while its sometimes painful to see our shortcomings, reflection helps us to constantly grow. And when we grow as supporters of play children benefit and that is our
highest goal!

A self-reflective practice of a playworker might look like this:

I'm thinking about a moment when Jenny and Sarah were playing inside that cardboard box. They were giggling and laughing, running in and out. I was just standing by enjoying their play when they asked me to cut a few windows so it would be lighter inside. I happily did and their play seemed to deepen because they could then look

out the window and interact with children outside the box. Billy and Samantha noticed this from afar and came closer to join in the fun. They all started playing some monster game. Lots of screaming. Then they asked me to be the monster and chase them around. Sure! "Raaaaar!" I chased them around to their delight and the game soon became to chase them around the yard and back into the box, then let them get out and chase them around and back to the box again.

This went on and on and I was really getting into it. I was roaring like a dinosaur and speaking in robot language. I was King Kong. I bumped it up a notch and started shaking the box every time they went back in. This was fun at first and then I guess I took it too far. Too much shaking? Too much roaring? They yelled "Stop!" and they all got out, giving me dirty looks. "You were supposed to be a friendly monster!" Sarah said as they walked out. Oops. I got so caught up in my monster persona that I misread their cues. I blew it! I stopped their play.

Sigh…..

Another scene might be like this:

Sally and Harmony were out in the wet grassy field putting straw into a bucket. The ground was really muddy and it looked like the bucket was filled with muddy water. They were having fun so I walked over to watch more closely. Harmony said they were making chocolate milk and needed a stick to stir it. I told them "no, you'll poke your eye out." They looked at me a little sadly, brought over a few more handfuls of straw and watched it sink in the bucket. They looked around again for a something to stir with, couldn't find anything and eventually wandered off. I think we have a rule that we don't play with sticks so I felt good about keeping them safe from the stirring stick. They really could poke an eye out you know!

After a bit of playwork training, this:

Sally and Harmony were at it again in the wet field, trying to make their "chocolate milk." They asked again for a stick to stir the concoction. This time I said ok. (In our playwork training we talked about how sometimes sticks are ok and my staff and I agreed that if sticks aren't being used as weapons we'd let them play with sticks. I didn't like it at first, and thought they could still poke their eye out, but this was the new rule so I went with it). I suggested we look in the garden to see if there were any scraps of wood they could use. Sure enough they found a small stick that would work and back they went to the bucket. They took turns stirring and getting more bits of straw for the mixture.

James noticed what they were doing and he came to join them. I've never seen them play with James before but they seemed fine with him helping them. He plopped in bits of ice. Three more girls came over and they had the idea of bringing the big barrel over to pour the mixture into. The bucket was heavy! But they worked together to lift it and successfully poured in the muddy water. Then they grabbed more buckets and began scooping water from puddles into the buckets and pouring that into the barrel. Then they had the idea of holding up one of the loose gutters, pouring the water into the gutter, watching it run down and splash into the barrel. That was a good idea, fun to watch the water run down the gutter. Then they had the idea of making a stand to hold the gutter so the girls didn't have to hold it by hand so they worked together to round up three tires, stack them up with a bucket on top and put the gutter on that. It was a little fragile but it worked! I just stood back and watched this whole thing. It was pretty cool.

More children came to check it out too. Then it was time to go inside but they left their construction still set up. I stuck around and watched the next batch of children come out. They noticed right away this neat-looking irrigation construction set up in the field. They started pouring water too. Then they knocked the gutter over and started pouring water on the tires. Then they knocked over the barrel and laughed with glee as the muddy water splashed out onto the ground. To tell you the truth, I was amazed at the play. It kept going on and on. There was great collaboration and an interesting mix of children included in the play. Everyone had a role and everyone's ideas seemed to be listened to.

I'm so glad I said yes to that initial stirring stick! I feel a little ashamed at saying no that time before. It totally stopped the play. I said no. The play stopped and none of those amazing things that happened on my "yes" day were able to happen. Not only did the initial play stop but the continued potential for play stopped too. I feel bad about that. But, I feel good about saying yes the next time and can really see how saying yes (but still keeping an eye on things) can really help play to happen. I am going to do that more.

There is a lot to know about the practice of playwork. It gets deep! We're just scratching the surface here. Thankfully there are lots of resources available to guide us, great folks to learn from, and lots of ways to incorporate playwork strategies into our work with children (there is a resource list in the Extra Stuff section of this book). Some good places to start are practicing *stepping back* and *observing* risky play before stepping in, being mindful not to *adulterate* the play with our adult agendas, and throughout it all doing *self-reflective practice* each day about the work we are doing and the new steps we are taking. Little by little. Step by step.
Day by day.

THE PLAYWORK PRINCIPLES

The Playwork Principles were drawn up by the Playwork Principles Scrutiny Group in 2004.[7]

These principles establish the professional and ethical framework for playwork and as such must be regarded as a whole. They describe what is unique about play and playwork, and provide the playwork perspective for working with children and young people. They are based on the recognition that children and young people's capacity for positive development will be enhanced if given access to the broadest range of environments and play opportunities.

1. Play is a biological, psychological and social necessity, and is fundamental to the healthy development and well-being of individuals and communities.

2. Play is a process that is freely chosen, personally directed and intrinsically motivated. That is, children and young people determine and control the content and intent of their play, by following their own instincts, ideas and interests, in their own way for their own reasons.

3. The prime focus and essence of playwork is to support and facilitate the play process and this should inform the development of play policy, strategy, training and education.

4. For playworkers, the play process takes precedence and playworkers act as advocates for play when engaging with adult-led agendas.

5. The role of the playworker is to support all children and young people in the creation of a space in which they can play.

6. The playworker's response to children and young people playing is based on a sound up-to-date knowledge of the play process, and reflective practice.

7. Playworkers recognise their own impact on the play space and also the impact of children and young people's play on the playworker.

8. Playworkers choose an intervention style that enables children and young people to extend their play. All playworker intervention must balance risk with the developmental benefit and well-being of children.

Rethink Your Rules

What if you could take a step back from your life with children and make up the rules that made the most sense to live by and let go of the rules that need not apply? What if you could reflect on your philosophies of outdoor play and your hopes and dreams for children's experiences and then craft new rules based on the things that really made sense for your children, your yard, your program?

Well, you can. While there are certain hard-fast national playground safety guidelines that playground equipment needs to adhere to, and licensing regulations that programs must follow, there are also whole sets of rules that you might be living by and enforcing that are more "in-house" rules—ideas passed down from years gone by that may or may no longer make sense. With the new way of thinking about risky play it could be high time to take a fresh look at your program's culture of play and start the conversations about why you do what you do and why you enforce what you enforce. The goal is to say no to children as little as possible.

How can we do that?

We can start by remembering that we are the ones making up the rules. We're the ones agreeing to them, following them, enforcing them. Yes, rules help us keep things running smoothly in life and in the play yard. Traffic would be a mess if we all drove on whatever side of the street we wanted to. Children need to know their boundaries for play.

But what if you have some rules that don't seem quite right? Can you think of any rules you enforce that feel outdated, restrictive, or limiting to children's free play possibilities? Since we're working to swing the pendulum back and allow more risky play, there might be rules that

RULES

What if you threw out **ALL** your rules?
What if you started over?

Some schools are doing just that:
no rules on the playground!

Other schools simplify it to three rules:

1. Respect others,
2. Respect yourself,
3. Respect the environment.

It really all boils down to that!

What would your simplest rules be?

get in the way. Now is the perfect time to rethink your rules and that starts by allowing yourself to ask some questions.

What rules of ours make sense and what rules don't? Why do we have this certain rule? Is this a government-enforced rule or is this our own rule? Is this rule for safety or is it to make the adults' job easier? Who came up with this rule? When, and why? Was it in reaction to an incident? Or was it based on someone's fear of an incident? Was it created because it feels like it "should" be a rule? Was the rule there before you started working there? Is it a rule that has been passed down from previous generations with no question? Then: what if it wasn't a rule? What might happen?? Would the world end? Would children implode? Would the adults implode? Or would life be easier and less full of "no's"?

All this questioning is healthy but it can also be tricky. Everyone has a different relationship to the rules. What makes sense to one person might feel restrictive to another. Someone might hate a rule that gives your world structure and meaning and you couldn't imagine not having that rule. *"Questioning that rule is like questioning my reality!"* And it's true. Rules become our reality.

But here's a secret: *we're making it all up as we go. Everything. Spoken or unspoken, we're collectively living by realities and rules we make up and agree on.*

So, let's make up the rules and realities we want to be living by! (And let's not let fears decide our realities.) But it can take time. Rethinking rules should happen slowly and carefully with compassionate conversations and deep listening. If it's just you making the decisions: great! Go for it! Lucky you. But most of the time rule-shifting needs to be a gentle but firm act of consensus-building. It could be scary for some folks to change. It could be

CULTURE OF PLAY

Like a mission statement or a set of bylaws it may be worthwhile for you to take a step back and consider the following:

- What is your culture of play?
- What are your goals for your children?
- What do you want them to experience?
- What is your philosophy about risky play and what is your commitment about incorporating it into children's lives?
- What is the adults' role in supporting play?

Questions like these can help you craft guiding principles to remind you of your mission and goals for outdoor play. From there you can build your play philosophy and practice. From there children can expand to their full potential. And from there anything is possible.

controversial. People's feelings about safety, fears, comfort levels, tradition, risks and responsibilities are not to be taken lightly. There could be disagreements. But if we truly want to make positive change in the lives of our children it is vital that we draw up the courage and have these challenging conversations. And *keep* having these conversations. And thank each other for being open to having these conversations. And you never know, people might be relieved. It might not be so difficult to make change after all. Sometimes it just takes asking the first questions to get it all going. What could you start to say yes to?

Environmental Choices

Just as we invent the rules that govern children's play, we adults also make the decisions about the *places* for children's play. **Do we want a natural playscape? Do we want rubber surfacing? Do we want a lot of fixed playground equipment or loose materials for children to build with?** Our culture of play informs our decisions about the play environment and what we want for our children. Are we shooting for safety? Or are we going for endless possibilities? Do we want children in a wild or manicured landscape? Natural materials or man-made? Wood or plastic? Rocks or boxes? Every playground is a reflection of the adults who envisioned it. Every yard shows their priorities.

What are your priorities? What do you want your children to experience? What materials do you want them to interact with? What are their possibilities for play?

The old way of thinking was that a playground meant equipment. A well-stocked playground was structures and pieces of play apparatus. But all that stuff tells children what to do and directs their play. The caregiving adults often have to spend time patrolling the equipment and enforcing the ways the equipment was designed to be used. The play can be enjoyable but clearly limited. The new way of thinking is to provide space and materials that say yes to play and let the children decide how to play and what to do. Instead of solid superstructures in the yard now people are adding flexible elements for children's creativity. They are building in risky areas, messy areas, places where children can do as they wish.

Now, a real child's space may look much less tidy than your average adult would appreciate. Your aesthetics may differ from children's "junkyard chic" but if it's really a place for play possibilities it's worth finding a compromise.

Here's an amazing environment I stumbled on during some travels. I can't say enough about this yard. I love the materials, the natural elements, and the connections to the surrounding landscape and what I appreciate most is the decision by the adults to make it what it is. There's a fire pit and sitting circle, a mud kitchen and a carpentry bench, but there's also a wildness and rawness. It's almost a forest school within the fenced-in area. The choices the adults made are the new way of thinking. The boulder, the little stream, the rocky terrain. The old way of thinking would probably have been to remove all this stuff. Redirect it. Place the fence in position to block it all out.

Instead these adults said we *want* the children to interact with this boulder. We *want* the water to flow in our yard. We *want* a challenging way to traverse the yard to get to the levels and plateaus beyond. These decisions weren't haphazard. They weren't by mistake. The adults here made clear conscious decisions to include (rather than exclude) these elements in their children's yard. It shows their values. They want children around natural materials. They want children to have some risky climbing opportunities. They want children to be a part of the seasonal flow of water. They think mess is ok.

They could have chosen otherwise. It took heavy equipment to clear the spot for the building construction and the machinery could easily have graded the hillside gently or plucked out the protruding rocks. They could have easily removed the tree and its root systems. The fence line could have easily been placed to block **out** the giant boulder and tiny waterway. But it was a clear decision to fence that stuff *in*. That's the new way of thinking. And yes it might be more work for the adults if the children get muddy trudging in the wet spot in spring. And yes they need to keep more of an eye on children scaling the rocks. And yes that's a big boulder there that children can climb and jump from. But this group wanted that. To them, the benefits outweigh the risks. The positive possibilities outweigh everything else. The space says yes, the adults say yes, and by the look of the "kid erosion" on the landscape the children say yes too.

And that was my happy thought walking back to my car in the parking lot. *This place really knows how to say yes.* As I walked along the sidewalk I noticed what at first looked like a small plumbing problem the school might be experiencing. There was a small hole dug, some ground disruption, and a discarded corrugated pipe. *Aw, that's too bad*, I thought. But as I came closer it became obvious that this was no plumbing issue and not made by the hands of adults. It was a project of children, right there in the middle of the yard. As I neared I saw hand tools left behind, rocks placed just so, and delicate small flowers lining the hole. It was beautiful. Amazing. Something special had gone on here. You could tell this small project was the center of some collaborative and determined effort. It was a delight to come across. And like a broken record I'll say it again: given the chance children will play. They will dig, climb, run, pretend, and build the neatest little flower-lined dug holes if we let them. And again I was impressed with the adults at this school. They were not saying no. They didn't say no to digging right here, right against the sidewalk, nearly in the middle of it all. They

didn't say no and when you don't say no you are saying yes. And when you say yes, beautiful things emerge. You're familiar with the saying, "Question Authority." Maybe you have a bumper sticker with that slogan on it. But as an adult working with children and wanting to support play it's important to **"Question your Authority."**

What do you say yes to? What do you say no to? What could you say yes to more of?

Clothing

One road block for letting children really get into the flow of play is the mess they may make while doing it. Some children don't like to get messy. Some prefer to stay neat and clean. But the majority of children care more about play than about total cleanliness. Let's face it, even while wearing fancified outfits it's hard to resist the chance to make a good mud pie. So what can we do to prevent the fear of mess from taking over and stopping play? How do we put systems in place to ensure that children can play freely without worrying about getting dirty? *What do we do about clothes?*

Lots of people have lots of strategies to take clean clothes out of the "saying no" equation. I've seen some creative solutions at childcare centers over the years. One strategy: promote your culture of play that celebrates creativity, exploration, and mess. Be known for it and partner with parents. Remember the term "play clothes?" That term is coming back! Groups are asking that children come to play in play clothes. That is, clothes that are ok to get dirty, grassy, muddy, wet, even a little torn. Not the fancy stuff. And, to have backup clothes on hand to change into if the first set gets too wet or dirty. Parents may supply these and you can keep them in cubbies. Some groups keep them neatly organized in zip lock bags each labeled with the name of the child-owner. Some programs require that backpacks are stocked daily with a change of clothes. Makes sense.

Other groups have huge bins filled with extra clothes not assigned to any specific child, perhaps just organized by size or gender. (Or not: I remember my son coming home from preschool in someone's else's pink snowpants on more than one occasion!)

These clothes could come from parents as hand-me-down donations. They could be extra clothes left by classes from long ago. Some groups take the burden off of parents and stock up at garage sales or ask for donations.

Now let's take it to the next level. Not only do we want to avoid improper clothes damping down daily play possibilities, we also don't want *fear* of clothes to stop any outdoor adventures. On rainy days, rather than groaning about the clothing hassles the rain will cause and keeping the children inside, having appropriate clothing on hand can enable a new kind of thinking: "Yay! Rain! Let's go outside and experience it!" But you can only do that if you have the proper clothing. As the saying goes, no bad weather, just bad clothing.

This also goes for *your* clothing, too. Too often it's the adults without rain gear or boots that keeps the fun inside. But I know you: you've got some great snow pants, right? Nothing's going to stop you. Right? So, step one is adults

dressing properly. No need for you to be cold outside! Step two is getting children properly outfitted for all outdoor conditions. Again, this goes along with your culture of play that states that children need to be outside every day in all conditions. If this is your school model then it will attract families that agree and dissuade families where that doesn't float their boat. So, there could be requirements for outdoor clothing for adventure play in all seasons. This means parkas, hats, gloves, rain boots, maybe winter boots depending on where you live, long underwear, rain pants, and snow pants. There are many clothing companies that make great children's adventure apparel. We don't want to exclude families who can't afford this gear so maybe there is a way to have the adventure clothing on hand available for all children to use.

Again, I love the forest school model. They have the kids in full body spacesuit-style head-to-toe rainsuits. There they are on hand ready for anybody who wants to get down and dirty. If mud is a real part of the experience (and if you live in a place that has spring it probably is) than you need some gear. Could you write a grant for it so that it is available for all? Could you crowd-source it so others can support children's playful explorations? Could you write a letter to a clothing company and ask for donations? Or seconds? The well-built stuff lasts for many years even with rough and tumble play.

So that's it. Start with basic play clothes that can take a little wear and tear and then bump it up to adventure suits that ensure that nothing—not weather, not mud puddles, not a skittish adult—is going to come between a child and their (muddy) play. And remember: this stuff can be hosed off! Mud cleans up. Children too!

No bad weather, just bad clothing!

Outdoor play has a long tradition in Nordic childcare. The Lyseth committee that made the first public report addressing Norwegian childcare in 1961 stated that **children should not play indoors for more than two hours at a time.**[8]

Working With Parents

Well, it's all fine and dandy to let your own children play risky or get messy but what if you're in charge of other people's kids?! You've got a responsibility. Parents might not share the same enthusiasm that you do about mess, risk, and outdoor play. What do you do then?

Some parents are obviously into risky nature play. Maybe that's why they were attracted to your program in the first place and always send their children to school with durable outdoor gear and are happy to see their kids dirty at the end of the day. Other parents like to dress their children up in fancy finery and expect them to come home as squeaky clean as they left. Other parents don't have the luxury or time for allowing clothes to get messed up. They might not have the money. Parents might also have different philosophies about play. They might have different worries. They may not understand the importance of free play. They may be concerned about school readiness and expecting to see worksheets for the children. Understandable. It's a competitive world out there.

Here's the thing: you can help educate parents about how your culture of play is supporting their children's wonderful growth and development. You can be a proponent for play. Let parents know that a dirty child is a creative, investigative child who problem-solves, has adventures with friends and is honing their preliteracy skills. Help them understand the connections between free play, risky play and brain development. Help them see that their children are having fun. And learning. And developing just the way they need to be. Their children will be ready for school. (Will school be ready for them?) And if their

children are already in school, I think most parents are all for more recess and freer, less stressful play periods.

If you need to, you can load them up with research and studies that promote play. There is a wealth of information you can share to back up your point of view and practice. If parents ask questions or are nervous about play elements, share your risk-benefit analysis process. Let them know how you are managing risks and minimizing injuries. Explain the difference between risks and hazards. Loan them this book! Making a drastic change to allow more risk and mess suddenly can be tough on parents who knew you and your program when it was cleaner and seemed safer. You might have to go slow with that first batch of families. It may indeed be true that this isn't what they signed up for. Their initial tour didn't have children in Norweigan rain suits sitting in mud puddles!

But it gets easier over time. Once you implement changes slowly and carefully with those first families everyone starts to get the idea that this is what you are all about. It actually does become clear from the initial parent tour that you value play, risk, and mess in a certain specific way. Parents immediately get the idea and YAY! And sign up. (Probably on the waiting list because this style of care is becoming so desirable!) Or they give each other funny looks, slowly back away and you never hear form them again. I've worked with schools that say that is absolutely fine with them. You want your program to match up with people who share your culture of play.

It's always good to strive to be on the same page with the parents and families you serve. Communication is the key. And celebration of what their children and your school are up to on a daily or weekly basis. Share pictures and stories. Post photo collages or projects. Offer them articles, books, and research that supports your philosophy of play. Soon enough you may find that you have a whole community of families that share and celebrate your philosophy of play.

Parent Newsletter #47

Mud, Glorious Mud!

Parents Beware: springtime is here! That means we are going to be starting up our nature walks again. Since there are lots of puddles along our path will be needing parents to send rubber boots to school.

Since we will be spending more time outside your little ones will also need old clothes that can get dirty. They have important work to do! At pick-up, please take time to check your child's cubby and look for wet or muddy clothes. Remember to replenish your child's extra clean clothes. Also, an old sweat shirt or light weight fleece would be nice to leave here for warmer days.

We have been gathering ideas to have more of our classroom time outside exploring nature, feeding birds, and planting seeds. Please stop and take a look at the slide show photos of our adventures on top of cubbies!

Thanks for being great parents!

PART 3
Provocatives

The World Is Upside Down

There is a Zen saying "the world is upside down." It means the way we look at the world is actually the complete opposite of what it really is. The idea is, somewhere along the line, we flipped the spiritual meaning of life. Instead of focusing on love, compassion, gratitude, awareness, and impermanence, we began focusing on the material world (jobs, wealth, things, etc.) and that desire for and chasing of those things has caused us great suffering. It is our journey to turn the world back right-side up.

I see that the same sort of thing has happened to our view of childhood, play, safety, and overprotecting. The world is upside down. Many of the things we worry about and eliminate are actually things we *want* for children's lives and should be standing up for. What was looked at as bad is actually good. It's more dangerous for children *not* to have "risky" things in their lives. Safety used to require removing risks. Now we know risk is important. Rules used to demand removing natural elements like rocks and roots from children's environments. Now we work to include those elements. Children have been segregated according to age, but now we know that mixing children of different ages is beneficial and important. Children used to be able to climb trees but now some rules say no. Children have been barefoot throughout human history but now regulations frown on it. Children like to wrestle and roughhouse, but now adults say no even as literature supports its practice. In so many cases what is truly good for children has been deemed unacceptable and the world has seemed upside down.
We lost our yes.

Now, dear reader, together we venture into territory that will help us all get the world right-side up again.

Together we stand to find ways to support what we know is right for children—to be mindful of our environments, to be thoughtful with our practices, to be vigilant in our supervision and support of play. And also to be confident in our voices. To have the difficult conversations. To work for new rules and ideas in our workplaces and in our hearts. To bring things right-side up again, it takes recognizing the upside down reality and saying, **"no more."** Time to take a stand and take a step. Even a small step is a step in the right direction. Each step to providing children with the opportunities for healthy play is a step that tilts the world right-side up.

In the last section we looked at ways to empower us to say yes more. In this section we'll look at a collection of things we want to say yes to! Based on the old way of thinking about risk and rules some of this stuff might feel edgy, provocative, even dangerous! Some of it is indeed risky but does that mean it should be removed from children's lives? The old way of thinking said so. The upside-down world views it that way. But those times are changing. If you want to bring opportunities for risky play back to your children, here are some things to include. Behind each idea and image are adults like you who have found ways to not say no. They have done risk-benefit analyses, brought in appropriate clothing, worked with licensors and accreditation, educated parents on the benefits, implemented risk- management techniques, all to feel comfortable saying yes and allowing children to say yes (or no) too. Each example is a way to make your environment richer, the choices for your children wider, and opportunities for healthy growth and safe risk-taking greater. Nothing you'll see is too outrageous. In fact, it's all perfectly normal in the right-side up world. Cheers to the good stuff. See you on the flip side!

Loose Parts

One of the simplest and least expensive ways to boost the fun and creativity in your outdoor space is to add "loose parts" for play. Loose parts can be anything such as cardboard boxes, kitchen pots and pans, blankets, tires, boards, traffic cones, milk crates, tennis balls, golf balls, ping pong balls, pine cones, branches, or seed pods. Loose parts can be almost anything. Children don't really care as long as they can build with it, create with it, make stuff with it. We all have our own aesthetics and sense of beauty. You decide what you want your space to be filled with. You can decide how you want it to look. Some folks like the "junkyard" feel of the adventure playground. Other people prefer keeping a playscape natural with all natural loose materials. That's fine too. **The important thing is that children have materials that allow them to change and re-create their environments according to their ideas and creativity.** Fixed playground equipment is fine and dandy. It's built tough and usually does what it was made for just fine. But children can't change it. Not really. But they can with loose parts. Every random tire is rich with possibility. Every straw bale can have a life of its own. The stuff is just waiting for the child to play with it.

Years ago my practical (and unique) father-in-law gave me a new rope as a housewarming gift. *"A thousand uses"*

he said mysteriously. It wasn't a gift you might expect. And yet I knew what he was getting at. Treated with care this single item could be used and reused infinitely for an infinite number of jobs and applications. The same goes for loose parts on the playground. A pirate themed playhouse is a pirate themed playhouse but a collection of boxes, tires, boards, straw bales and rope(!) can become a play house, an obstacle course, a space ship, school, a car, a boat, a living room, a pool, a clubhouse. You get the idea. We could fill the rest of this book with a list of things children could make from that stuff. That's what we want for our children: endless possibilities.

Simon Nicholson said in his Theory of Loose Parts, *"In any environment, both the degree of inventiveness and creativity, and the possibility of discovery, are directly proportional to the number and kind of variables in it."* [9] If we believed that we'd have our playgrounds filled not with fixed equipment but instead with high numbers of loose things to spark the good stuff he's referring to. You probably do this already. Children in classrooms and living rooms around the world build all sorts of amazing things with building blocks and couch cushions that we'd never imagine. Yes, they are learning math and science

and engineering but they are also simply following their whims and molding their reality according to their own wishes.

It's an adult-dominated world for children, let's face it. They play when we say they can and with what we give them to play with. We tell them when to brush their teeth, when to line up, when to take naps, what is polite to say, and what is impolite to say.

Loose parts offer children the chance for a little autonomy and freedom. It's a chance for the child to have control over their surroundings. That's a breath of fresh air. It's a chance to be free. It's a chance to delve into something and see where it takes them. It's a chance for the child to make the decisions. It's a chance to collaborate. It's a chance to create their own stories and mythology. It's a chance to be creator!

And it's also a chance to be destroyer. That's part of the fun too, right? It's an important part of play that we sometimes overlook. Loose parts let it all happen. Loose parts provide opportunities for fun and creativity on many levels. First there is the creativity and possible collaborations on designing, building and constructing some object with loose materials. Then there is the actual play that could occur in and around whatever the children built. School bus, fairy hut, bear's den, space station. Then as it plays out there is the destroying of whatever you built. Yaaaaaaaah! If everyone is on board with the destroying, it's fun to watch your world safely crumble to the ground.

Tibetan monks practice a form of devotional meditation by spending weeks painstakingly creating intricate and beautiful sand-painting mandala works of art, grain by colorful grain, then say prayerful blessings and ceremoniously destroy the whole thing. In the same way, the creation and destruction of loose parts play creations too is a meditation and firsthand experience of the law of impermanence. Everything changes. **Play is children living in the ever-present now. They see how water flows, how leaves fall and witness first hand that nothing stays the same.** That's deep stuff right there, in the midst of fun and games. It's a nice thing to learn when you are the one in control.

Provocatives 79

Loose parts let children control their play and build what they want to build. It's not for us to determine the outcome, but rather to simply provide the stuff, the raw materials. We could never imagine what empowered children may create with the junk that we've given them. It's another one of those "stand back and be amazed" opportunities. You can predict that children will use the stuff, but you can never fully predict how. The beauty of playful surprises!

I remember a time when a well-meaning adult dropped off a pile of plastic quart containers to a play day I was staffing. I thought, *"Uh, what are kids going to do with those? They're plastic. They'll probably break. I bet nobody will be into those very much."* And sure enough I was proven wrong almost instantly when the children arrived, built an elaborate banquet table with tablecloth, place settings, candelabras, seating and yes, those plastic cups filled with muddy water as the center piece of their play as sacred chalice-goblets that each child said blessings over to start their make-believe feast! It had nothing to do with my limited taste or creativity!

What kinds of loose parts should you use and where do you get them? **It almost doesn't matter what stuff you put out for play, just that you put it out there.** You want loose parts that are relatively safe, no sharp edges or toxic materials obviously. Age-appropriateness is important of course as well as how much room you have to store the stuff. But it really comes down to what you can get your hands on. Every play space could be filled with different materials depending on the community and specifics of the place. If you are a nature-based program or live in the woods sticks become your materials. If you

are in the tropics it might be palm fronds and coconuts. If you are in town or an urban area wood can come from tree service contractors or your city forester. Furniture and appliance stores are great suppliers of boxes. Second hand stores and reuse centers are treasure troves for loose parts. Gutters, plastic tubing, pulleys, wheels, frisbees, balls.

Do you live in a place that manufactures special products? If so they may have acceptable "seconds" or scrap materials that are a by-product of what they make that could serve your purposes. I've seen some interesting collections of play-appropriate industrial materials including truck loads of weird plywood cut-out shapes, spools of mis-colored climbing rope, leftover ladder parts. I did a playground project once in a town that was home to a large windchime factory! They had an endless supply of mistuned chimes, discontinued chimes and every wooden piece of a windchime set that you could ever imagine. When I was a kid my town was home to a wooden toy train company and once every so often they'd open their garage doors early on a Saturday morning and the public was invited to come in and grab what they wanted from seconds bins. So I was lucky enough to grow up surrounded by beautiful maple blocks, half-made train cars, and a million little wooden wheels. I had so many I could glue them together and made spaceships, skyscrapers, and houses for my cat. Check with your local widget factory down the road to see what they may have for you! And put the word out to friends, neighbors, and other parents to see what odd stuff they may be able to donate to the cause when they clean out their garages or pull out beat up pots and pans from their kitchens.

Stuff Says Yes

Did you know that loose parts talk to children? It's true. Just like we adults say yes or no, the materials and stuff we provide for children say yes or no too. I admit it: I used to be a nature purist. I only wanted beautiful natural things in children's environments. A worn-out tire in a child's playground was beneath my idea of what we should offer our children…until I saw a huge assortment of tires being used by children as loose play parts. Oh. Wow. Ok.

Instantly I changed my tune as I saw tractor, truck, and car tires being used by a single group of kids to build huge sculptures, castles, rolling tire games and more. My yes was expanded. And one of the things I like about tires and recycled used materials is that they too say yes to children. If a thing is too precious, too beautiful, too obviously loved by the adults it sends a message that it should really only be used in certain ways: the adults aren't going to want me wrecking this stuff. I better be careful. Whereas, loose parts that are a little beat up, a tire, scrap boards, used colanders, or tennis balls in abundance say to the child, *"Use me how you'd like to. Do whatever you want. The adults know I'm here but they've put me here for you. Be creative!"* When we're working our best to say yes to children the stuff we supply should say yes too.

84 Adventures in Risky Play

Beauty is in the eye of the beholder and in this case the beholders are children. And the things they are beholding look different to us than they do to them. That muddy plastic cup banquet table to the adults looked like the junk we had set out earlier only nicely arranged. But to the banquet-goers it could have been as fancy as a table set for the Queen of England. Through the eyes of a child straw bales, boxes and boards are transformed into the stuff of legendary stories. They may not even see the cardboard as they are zooming to Mars or the bottom of the sea. It's all a means to a make-believe end. It eventually transforms back into the ordinary but for moments it's magic. If we learn how to look and fully say yes we'll see it too.

To others with a slightly different vantage point could this be chaos? Anarchy? A disaster waiting to happen? With loose parts anything can happen so part of your risk management scheme is to keep a somewhat close eye on things and even establish some basic ground rules. Talk it over with your children. Invite their ideas of how to most appropriately use the stuff. They know deep down the lines they shouldn't cross. That doesn't mean you shouldn't still keep careful watch on things. Lines do occasionally get crossed! Adding this stuff definitely makes the play more interesting but it also means your job might be busier too. You'll want to make frequent safety checks on all your pieces and parts to make sure nothing has become hazardous overnight (or after a wild spaceship-destructing

session). Decide where the best places for your loose parts will be and if there are any places loose parts should not be used. Some groups leave their stuff out and don't mind a messy environment. Other people prefer tidiness or share the space with others, or are in a public place where loose stuff could walk away at night.

Having good storage is often the key to having good loose parts play. It can be fun to rotate the loose stuff, stage different areas with different materials to keep the space interesting and full of surprises. That is one of the fun roles of a playworker. A spacious storage shed lets you stockpile your stuff and dish it out in bits over time. Or your storage shed can be open for the children to grab what they want when they want to. Or perhaps you have smaller satellite storage spots in specific locations in the yard. Sand parts near sand pits. Water play stuff near the fountain. Digging tools stored by the giant dirt hill. Or maybe you're free to leave it all out in a celebrated mess. Again, it doesn't matter exactly how you provide the loose parts for play, just that you provide them.

86 Adventures in Risky Play

Hiding

Children love to run, climb and build outside but they also love hiding away. There's nothing quite like a good hidey nook to hunker down in and spy out of. We all have times when we need to get away from it all for some alone time and perspective. Children need that too—especially if they have been cooped up with adults for a long time! They need some time on their own. They need some privacy. They need hiding places. They need spots outside where they can feel like nobody can see them, even if they can still look out and see the world. Most children love to get into small private spaces whether it's behind a row of shrubs, inside a clump of tall grasses, or beneath some fixed playground equipment.

You've heard the word *"claustrophobia"*—the fear and dislike of being inside small, confined spaces. (Maybe you're claustrophobic?) Well, most children are just the opposite: they have a *love* of being in small, confined spaces. That's called "*claustrophilia*." You could call children "*claustrophiliacs*." They seek those small spaces out. For them it's fun and feels good. The fact that kids around the world seek out small hiding areas is an example of the *universality of play*. It's part of being human. From the adults' view it may simply look like a fun thing to do. But a deeper look may show that hiding is a hard-wired evolutionary safety mechanism to help children keep away from predators and those that would do them harm. Scary kids' movies always have kids outwitting bad guys by hiding away out of sight until the danger has passed. For kids in actual dangerous situations it's an important skill to have. But in the meantime hiding during play is just a fun and natural thing to do. We adults need to provide spots and spaces where children can hide.

But wait a second. Regulations might not let you do that, right? Then again, exactly where in your regulations does it say "Do NOT let kids hide?" Health and safety regulations want to keep children safe. They want you to be able to supervise your children. You want that too.

However, even the best-intentioned rules can leave themselves open for narrow interpretations and upside-down thinking with children suffering the consequences. Some regulations describe supervision as needing to *see* your children at all times. That mostly makes sense, but some licensors could interpret those regulations so strictly as to not let children hide and to force programs or schools to remove any and all hiding spaces, obstructions, plants, or structures that could block a complete view of every child on every part of a play area at all times. I've heard numerous accounts of a school that had wonderful bushes that kids loved to get inside of, only to be forced to remove them or trim them beyond recognition. "*Gotta see kids at all times,*" they say.

But do you really? What's the spirit of that regulation? I'd say it simply means you need to be able to supervise your children. You need to be able to know where they are and what they are doing. I agree. But does it mean that you have to *see* them at all times? Actually see everybody

and everything *at all times*? You would have to be nearly super-human to achieve that literally, or your play space would need to be a very flat and dull play environment.

How about this: what if we agree that children of certain ages need to be supervised and that adults need to generally know what's happening at all times. That sounds pretty good. What if it's not all about seeing? We have five senses after all! What if our rules added two simple words to the regulation language? What if the rules said, "Children must be supervised and seen *or heard* at all times?" That could make all the difference. If there's giggling coming from behind a fallen log, that should be enough. You know who's back there. You know what's happening. If you wanted to really see you could get closer or change your vantage point. Let that fall to the adults. There are many ways to supervise children.

But it might not just be regulators that are limiting hidey nooks. You might have fears yourself about children hiding away. I mean, what could they be doing in there?! Our imaginations can get away from us if we're not careful. So in the spirit of being careful and not letting our fears appear too real (and stopping play if it doesn't need stopping) why not run a risk-benefit analysis of hiding situations in your yard. It will help you determine if you think the hiding is ok or not. **What are the risks?** *Could a child actually get hurt in a hiding spot? Is it truly dangerous? Could they get stuck? And then how likely is it that something bad could happen in there?* **What are the benefits?** *Some privacy. Part of imaginative play. Bonding for friends hiding together, fun to spy out of. Crouching down is good for building core strength, etc.*

Perhaps the most important part of a hiding analysis is the *management* section: what are you going to do about it? How are you going to stay intentional about having a hiding spot or two, but still being able to supervise? This is your plan and proof to regulators that all this is intentional. They don't need to point out that you have places on your playscape where children can hide. You planned it that way! You've weighed the pros and cons, looked at the risks and benefits, determined that the benefits outweigh the health risks, and you've developed strategies to manage the spaces. Nice job!

"A good hiding space is where I can see the teachers, but they can't see me."

Provocatives 91

HIDING IDEAS

There are lots of ways you can manage to have hiding in your yard that will make you feel more comfortable *and* meet goals of regulations. Sometimes it's finding the perfect line of site for the adult caregiver so they can clearly see around the yard. Maybe there are strategic spots to stand with all the right angles or an elevated hill so you can see from above the fray. Other times its clever trimming of bushes to make them feel like good hiding places, but open enough to see inside. Children don't have to be fully hidden to still feel safe and sneaky. Give them a hint of being able to feel secluded. They'll take it from there. I've seen groups make great use of plastic mirrors on their playground to help adults see who might be behind a shed or around a corner. You could add chimes or musical instruments in hidden areas so you'll be able to hear when children are playing in secluded spots. Build hiding huts with window openings or slatted sides so you can see who's inside. A playhouse doesn't have to be fully enclosed for a child to feel hidden away. Partial walls or picket fence sides can do the trick for both the child who wants some privacy and for the adult who needs to see inside.

You can also say, *"I want children to be able to hide and I don't need to see in at all!"* Well, good for you. You can work to build in actual hiding locations with a variety of materials. I like the natural plant-style of hiding places but any hiding place is good. You could plant tall, soft ornamental grasses and a variety of shrubs. Leave some spaces between the plants and the fence or building for kids to run behind. Add cardboard boxes now and then with portholes to peer in and out of. Let kids hangout under the slide or fixed play structure. Think about the corners of your yard and how a single plant or shrub could

make them feel private to a child tucked in behind on a log bench. Provide loose parts and let children build their own awesome hiding spots. Once you decide that hiding is important there are a million ways you can do it. It doesn't matter how. It just matters that children get to hide.

SIGHT AND SOUND

Australian Early Childhood Guide to the National Quality Standard states that children be *"supervised in all areas of the service, by being in sight and/or hearing of an educator at all times..."* Makes sense to me! [10]

Fire

Fire and young children? Are you crazy?! Maybe that's your first reaction to the idea of fires on the playground. When we think a little further we remember that children have been around fire for thousands of years. Fire is an important part of our human history. Like earth, water, and air, fire is elemental. As we strive to let children grow and learn in the real world, it's important that we connect them to the authentic elements on our planet. Children are endlessly mesmerized and fascinated by fire. It glows, dances, changes color, appears to be alive. It has personality, strength, energy and must be respected. Like the other earth elements, even the tiniest bit of fire in the flame of a candle is part of the whole. As adults we're still fascinated by fire. It's mysterious and beautiful. And it needs to be treated with care. It's not something to take lightly or act foolishly around. We learned that as children. How do our children learn that today? I think the best way for children to learn about fire and fire safety is in the company of caring adults. Like you. For children's long-term safety they depend on us to teach them about fire. Like crossing the street, or riding a bike, or climbing a tree, the only way to truly learn about fire is to be around it.

Do you remember being around fires when you were a child? *Oh yeah, I loved cooking hotdogs over fires.*
Roasting marshmallows. S'mores! We had campfires when I was growing up. I guess that's not so crazy. We cook over fires. Fires keep us warm in cold weather. Dragons breathe fire. Fires light up the dark. I loved the fireplace in my home growing up. And I love sitting around a fire with family, friends and children. Watch the babies, keep your eye on the toddlers, but when children are ready they can absolutely be trusted to be careful and safe around fire. They can feel its heat and power from a distance and know it is nothing to be taken lightly. Besides being with my own family and friends having bonfires with children, the first time I saw open fires in an educational setting was while visiting nature kindergartens in Scotland. They had it down. Risk-benefit analysis of fires, safety management of fires, rules worked out with children around fires and then simple enjoyment with their fires. The children loved it. Seeing the children around the fire just felt like a natural part of a normal day.

Since that Scotland visit I've learned of programs all over that have seen the (fire) light and have found ways to incorporate fires into their days. Yes, forest schools and nature kindergartens. But also licensed, accredited, childcare centers and preschools are doing fires within their fenced-in playgrounds in urban and suburban neighborhoods.

LESLEY ROMANOFF, Director
Takoma Park Cooperative Preschool
Takoma Park, Maryland, United States

Why is it important for you to have fires outside with children? What do you like about it?
Our parent cooperative school recently celebrated its 75th year. The way we look at our practice is that we owe it to the founders and the parents who have gone before to make sure childhood, and all its adventures, are preserved and continued into the future. We have found that this sometimes means making certain things available—things that we ourselves experienced when we were children. These include running as fast as you can across a field, sledding, rolling down hills, climbing trees, floating boats, and building fires. These opportunities hold as much importance in our educational program as anything else we offer.

We have monthly parent meetings and at least one of these meetings we hold a campfire at the school. We also have regular campfires, regardless of the weather in heat and in rain or snow, for the children. What I like best about campfires is that they call to us with story. It is a primal experience that pulls us together. We cook at these campfires and we share stories. The greatest joy is when the children begin to tell the stories. They lean forward, eyes glowing, hands raised, sharing something they all know to be true and also completely made up.

Another thing I really like about the campfires is that the fires themselves create yet more loose parts... charcoal, ashes, and burned sticks become precious resources for mark making, potion brewing, and fairy dust. So many uses!

What do the children think about the fires?
The children are fascinated, of course. Our goal is to create a healthy respect and confidence around fire and cooking with fire. The joy on their faces when they are able to either keep a branch lit or light the fire themselves along with maintaining it is irreplaceable. They also learn patience. Nothing can be rushed, from selecting the perfect kindling, to turning the logs, and waiting while their food sizzles and cooks (or burns).

How do you manage fire? What is a typical fire scene? How do you keep it safe?
We have several fire pits, although the children will build individual fires on bricks or in the sand pit. For a group campfire, the older children built a brick and stone lined pit and we use that. This pit has a ring of logs around it. The children are taught to walk well around the center when the fire is going, but this pit is also simply there when the children are playing outside. I feel that this is important because it helps children internalize its location, its surroundings, and its meaning during their play.

We have a campfire kit in a bin, which includes cooking materials like tongs, hot pads, and foil. We also have a collection of fire starters (lint, stick bundles, etc.) in the bin, and a fire blanket as a safety precaution.

How did you teach children about fire?
The teaching about fire begins with active participation such as picking up kindling and joining in the effort of stacking the wood for the fire. We have been doing this for a long time and the one thing that seems to be consistent is that children have a common sense approach and respect for fire. I believe that this is because fire is hot and they can feel this heat. They can see it. And the smoke of the fire is something that moves in advance of the flame so that is a good cue too. With our little ones, the three- and four-year-olds, we hold to the practice of walking around the log ring (outside of the fire ring) because they are more likely to trip and fall and better to do this away from the fire.

What are your safety rules around fire? Do's / don'ts?
We put our fires out with sand not water. Asking people how they put out fires is always a big laugh for me because people have very strong opinions about it. The reason I do this is that it preserves the quality of the loose parts (ash, charcoal sticks, burned logs) and reduces the amount of smoke in the air. But because we use sand, adults do need to check it the next day before children play in the yard to make sure that all the heat has dissipated. This is an additional safety precaution we have in place. The children can light branches/sticks on fire but they must keep them in the fire ring.

What is your advice to others wanting to try having fires?
My advice would be to hold a campfire session with parents during the evening. By bringing them together to tell stories, cook food, and share memories your work will already be done. Start small, with popcorn over a fire. I don't like commercial metal fire pits because they get hot to the touch and are more likely to be touched. Begin sharing recipes and memories; these are the connective threads that bring us together.

Anything else?
I really, really, really want a tripod with a hanging cast iron pot and kettle. And I don't want to buy it. We have a parent who is a welder so stay tuned!

Pretty inspiring! Could you do this too? Maybe you start small and try it as a one-time event. You could celebrate a summer holiday with a family cookout or hold a Winter Solstice Celebration around the light of a fire. Maybe there are some parents who can be your fire tenders and fire safety volunteers. My son's preschool had a dad who specialized in teaching traditional wilderness skills come in to teach the children about fire and how to make fire by friction, no matches. Or maybe you just have a fire pit for *pretend* fires. Children can put sticks and pine cones in the fire pit and imagine lighting a big blaze. Pretend s'mores aren't *quite* as good as the real thing, but…

PHOTOS COURTESY OF TAKOMA PARK COOP

98   Adventures in Risky Play

Provocatives

Water

We all know children love water. If there's a puddle to jump in they'll find it. If there is some water and cups to pour and dump, they'll pour it. If there is a body of water they'll throw a rock in it. Splish splash. It's another one of those universal truths of childhood. Water sparks something deep inside the child. Like fire, water is elemental and mesmerizing. How does it move? How does it splash? How does it react to my actions? It's one of the ultimate loose parts and a constant science experiment and fascination for children. I don't need to hype up water— you know all this is true.

But the question may be, how do you "do" water? How do you meet licensing requirements? How do you keep kids from getting soaked? How to you manage wet clothes and wet surfaces? Like all these topics, it's worth working through and finding a solution so children have the opportunity to play with water.

Water could be a sprinkler, a hose, a water table. It could be a farm pump, a fountain, or a small trickle down a backyard water feature. It could be a rain barrel, a watering can, a squirt bottle or spritzer. It could be the downspouts of your home on a rainy day or the puddle left behind when the snows finally melt. Children would appreciate any of these opportunities to touch water and work with its magical qualities. Water with sand takes everything to a higher level with kid civil engineering projects of rivers, creeks, dams, and floods. Watering garden plants reminds us that all life needs water to live and grow. A drinking fountain quenches our own thirsts. So many possibilities, so many means to the end: children + water.

"But licensing won't let us have water," I've heard it said more than once. We know that regulations have thoughts on water in children's spaces. We know they want to keep children safe. But if we take a close look at regulations or ask a follow-up question we find out the greater truths. Such as: you can't have *standing* water. You can't have water more than a certain small depth. That might rule out kiddie pools and goldfish ponds but it doesn't mean no water at all! It's our job as adults to know the guidelines and rules that affect our worlds. It's our job to have conversations with regulators and ask the follow-up questions. **Remember: when it comes to creating beautiful worlds for our children, there is always a way to say yes.**

We can adjust our dreams to fit the guidelines. We can alter the details to pass regulations. A teeny water flow from a hose in a shallow sandy ditch might not feel as exciting to us adults as a beautifully landscaped backyard creek with pools and multiple wading spots but children don't mind. The teeny water flow holds a world of possibilities. It's water! It's moving! It's alive! Then it disappears in the ground. That is very exciting. Endless possibilities and interest! Don't let your adult scale and perspective stop you from being happy with tiny ways for water in your yard. If the rules say you can't have standing water, don't let it stand. If they say you can't have any deep water that pools up, don't! If you can be flexible you can be open to a world of possibilities for children who might never know what they are missing. (And seriously - it's more fun to spray children with a garden hose on a hot day than just watch them in a small kiddie pool, right?)

And at the same time, take children to bigger water. Let them see creeks, rivers, lakes, oceans. Let them be in the the presence of water and feel its essence. It's grand to come in contact with a larger body of water. The big water moves and makes patterns and rings just like the water in your water table. Let children feel that connection. Many nature preschools and neighborhood childcare centers take field trips to water. Some have their very own ponds and creeks on site outside the fenced-in playground. All seasons are interesting for study of a wetland. All weather teaches us that we are part of a greater whole. There is a system that surrounds us with rain, clouds, rivers, the sea. We are a tiny part of the cycles of water on our planet. It's beautiful. The earth—nurturing and cleansing itself constantly. We're lucky our planet has water, you know! Maybe children know that already. Maybe that's why they feel a kinship with the elements. Maybe that's why water feels like their friend. Don't break up that potential friendship! Find your ways of having water. Find your flow.

Provocatives 105

106 Adventures in Risky Play

Mud

Another great thing about children? They're completely washable! Even the muddiest kid can eventually get clean. And the muddiest clothes, well, they can get mostly clean. Or replaced! Some people spend a lot of time and energy trying to keep children clean. I often feel sorry for those adults—and those kids. It's hard to stay clean when there's so much playing to do! I hate to think of children's play limited by worries about getting dirty—either by adults saying no or children *imagining* adults will say no. It's sad to think about children caught in the midst of play stopping to listen to adult voices in their heads disapproving or shaming them for getting messy. We know adults can adulterate play. But what is it called when adults (parents, teachers, etc.) adulterate the play without even being there? When children stop their play because they've internalized adults' "no's"? "My mom is going to be mad," says the girl looking down at her now-muddy coat after doing some amazing play with friends. Or "My dad will kill me if I get these sneakers dirty."

But we're here to talk about "yes-ing" our "no's." Mud and muddiness is often a no. It's muddy! Icky! Gooey! Dirty! But, it's also fun and squishy, squirty, slippery and slimy. No wonder so many children love it. Adults pay big bucks to get mud spa treatments for face and body. Every gardener knows how good it feels to have their hands in the dirt; science now tells us why: dirt has been shown to contain "happy microbes" that spark the brain to produce more serotonin that helps you feel more relaxed and happier in the same way that anti-depressant drugs do. Oh, how nice! That's a good reason we should all be barefoot more often and why we should play in mud!

We've talked about clothes being key to muddy play but what could mud play look like? It could be simple like mud in a sensory table for hands-on squishing. (Here's the basic mud recipe: dirt + water = mud!) You could keep things semi-cleanish with children wearing aprons to protect their clothes from mess. Add simple tools to bump up the fun like spoons, cups, bowls, and funnels. Take things to the next level and try out the famous "mud kitchen." Counter space, dirt, water, pots and pans. Some children really want visceral play with stomping and splashing in mud. Nature schools that take kids to the woods do this kind of thing every day. Clothes help, but mostly it's the attitude of the adults. Dirtiness is secondary to the play. They might not even think about the children getting dirty because they consider it a normal part of the day.

Getting dirty is like breathing for these supportive adults; natural, normal, and necessary. Getting muddy is really just a by-product of play. A by-product of being a child! If the children don't mind getting dirty, if there's no adult in their head or adults in real life making them feel bad about getting dirty, their play can just flow where it wants to go. It's really an attitude shift for adults. If we question our cleanliness motives it might really be about *us*. Mud on children is just a way of life, but that way of life makes our life more difficult!

What if we simply saw it as "what is" and then "what we're doing next" (cleaning up)? It's not more work. It's just our work.

And if we start to allow it, we start to soften the harsh voices of criticism. When we observe with compassionate caring hearts and see the amazing play and growth and learning that happens when we say yes, we can see the clean up, wash-up and the de-dirtying as an offering to the beauty and power of play. We can think of it as devotional practice in service to the spirit of play and childhood. And when we devote ourselves with open hearts that too produces serotonin and we relax and feel happier. (Children pick up on those good vibes too.) And if we devote ourselves while standing in mud, lookout! Love and happiness are in the air!

LEVI'S MUDDY BUTT STORY

I was stopping by my older son's preschool and I had my two-year-old son Levi with me. The preschool, with its endless supply of loose parts, art materials, nature, books and fun-loving big kids was like a magical kingdom for the little guy and he loved to stop by for visits and explorations. It must have been a day after a rain because the ground was soft and soggy with lots of muddy puddles. Sure enough with my back turned Levi found a nice mud patch, stood in it, then slipped in it. Plop! He doesn't like his hands to get muddy so I helped him up, wiped his hands, and surveyed the outcome, much to his older brother's delight: muddy butt!

I had a series of reactions, both professional and parental. First was *"Haha pretty cute and funny."* The second was *"Oh no what a mess! How are we going to deal with this?"* Then, worrying, *"I don't have extra clothes with me. We've got to get back in the car at some point! Am I going to get muddy? The car seat muddy? The car muddy?? What am I going to do?"* (All with Levi still happily standing in the mud.)

Then I had a talk with myself, *"Ok, Keeler, Mr. 'Mud Advocate', what are you going to do now? Put your money where your mouth is, buddy. You can't look people in the eye and say they should deal with muddy kids if you can't!"* So, laughing to myself, I took some deep breaths, reassured myself that everything would be ok, brainstormed a little bit about logistics and let the play continue. What's the worst thing that could happen—strip Levi down and he'd ride home in his carseat in his diaper? Not the end of the world. And that is exactly what we did.

And yes, I know that a single child getting muddy is far different than a whole classroom of children getting muddy. But that was me having a parental mud-moment like everyone else. I can feel your pain! Honestly, I'd rather not have to deal with the muddy butt. But, in the service of play and freedom that's our job. Take deep breaths, smile, let the serotonin flow and do what you gotta do. The adult's role ain't always glamorous, but it's all in the service of play.

NEW ZEALAND
MARVELOUS MUD STORY

So there I was, minding my own business at the Open Spaces Preschool in Whangarei, New Zealand. Their play area, like the school itself, is a great combination of natural materials, plants, sculpture, kid-built structures - and chickens! One feature I had noticed the day before was a small plot of dirt surrounded by smooth boulders next to the sand play area. I had been adding "dirt digging" areas next to "sand digging" spaces to spice up the fun in my own designs, so I was pleased to see their cute little dirt space. How nice. This time however, when I walked over to the dirt area something very interesting was happening: a teacher and a four-year-old girl had a hose spilling a trickle of water into the dirt. "Delightful," I thought. "Making a bit of mud." I watched the fun for a little while then went back to the school to charge my camera and eat a snack. After enjoying apple wedges and crackers and helping some boys make giant paper airplanes, I noticed some commotion coming from the sand/dirt area. I grabbed my camera and trotted over to find... the most amazing natural preschool mud play I had ever seen.

Oh... my... gosh! I couldn't believe my eyes and I couldn't help but smile and laugh. Here were six preschoolers stripped down to tee shirts and underpants slipping, slopping, and sliding in the dirt spot which had now become the most lovely, silky-smooth deep-brown mud ever. Glorious, delicious, delirious mud. Complete with children jumping in it, pouring it, dipping their hands in it, laying in it, and most of all laughing in it. Thank goodness my camera batteries had a little bit of juice left in them! With an amused caregiver standing by, these children were freely having the time of their lives. I honestly have never seen a playscape "feature" so loved and enjoyed in such a full-bodied, full-spirited way.

When the kids were done and ready to move on to something else I followed along to see what would happen next. *"How will the school deal with THIS mess?"* I wondered. And sure enough, they handled it with simplicity, common sense, and love... and a sense of humor: they hosed the kids down of course! When the squeals of delight subsided and everybody was hosed to an acceptable level of cleanliness, each child was wrapped tightly in a cozy, soft towel to dry. And when they were dry: clean clothes, shoes and socks back on, and over to the snack table for some yummy treats. Life doesn't get much better than that, does it?

So what is their secret? As an American I wondered: is that something that only New Zealanders are allowed to do? Only for preschools in the southern hemisphere?! Nonsense! There is mud all over the planet and there are children who love to get muddy all over the planet.

All it takes is some creativity, trust, and a spirit of play. The folks at Open Spaces Preschool have lots of extra clothes on hand plus parents who know and honor the benefits of free play—even messy play. I talked with one dad who said he always knows when his daughter has had a lot of fun at school because there is dirt behind her ears!

So how can you try this? What would it take? As far as playscape design goes it's certainly simple. Perhaps you are already blessed with rich soil in your yards that you could expose with some turf or pavement removal. Or maybe you need to get a load of soft fluffy topsoil delivered to make a "mud mound." Always be sure to pick through the soil and remove any sharp stones or unwanted debris, of course. You'll also want a water source of some kind to make the mud, and clean up muddy kids. It's really just about designating a space, and allowing it to happen. It's about giving yourself and your children permission to do it. To do what children have always naturally done.

Mud Kitchens

When people ask me what's the biggest trend in children's outdoor play spaces I say mud kitchens! When people ask me what's the simplest way to take your play space to a higher level I say mud kitchens! I really do. If you put some kind of a table in your yard plus a variety of pots and pans, plus some water and/or just loose fill materials like dirt or sand or flower petals to play with, children will be absolutely drawn to it. They can't help it. A mud kitchen by its very nature is a feature that says "yes."
Yes you can play, yes you can make mixtures, yes you can concoct, yes you can create, yes you can make a mess, yes you can!

A mud kitchen is ideal for experiments and discoveries. It's made for mixing and making: soups and poisons, hot chocolates and cakes. It can all happen at the mud kitchen. Why? Is it because it suggests you have freedom to play around? Is it because the mud kitchen is an extension of the beloved indoor sensory table? Is it because the mud kitchen seems to say a little mess is ok? Is it a more refined way of playing with sand if you don't need to put your whole body into it? Is it tapping a subconscious draw to food-making and survival? Is it role-playing like mom, dad, or gramma in the kitchen? Is it a first window to the world of loose parts and endless child-led possibilities? Is it a place that feels more like a child's than an adult's—like the adults might just stay away because the mixtures look yucky? The short answer to it all is: yes. It might even be doubly attractive to children because it feels like a child's place rather than an adult's. Maybe it appears to have purpose for children who like to focus. Maybe it offers a chance to zone out, calm down, and stir, stir, stir. It's all good. And I'm telling you: you could have the most standard-seeming man-made playground, but if you set up a small table with loose mud kitcheny stuff in one corner, it transforms everything. One small step for you, one giant leap for your children's play and potential.

And as I'm saying over and over, it doesn't matter exactly how you execute the final design and creation. It just matters that you give it a try and get something happening out there. People are doing mud kitchens in a million different ways. It seems to be a popular DIY

project that can be simple or complex depending on your building skills, your budget, your materials, and what your end result wants to be. I've seen some big budget mud kitchens, some even made by commercial manufacturers, but for the most part mud kitchens are built by people like you and your friends and community members with the materials you might already have on hand. You got boards? You got a mud kitchen. You got some pots and pans? You've got a mud kitchen. Someone has an actual kitchen sink? Plop it in the mud kitchen.

My sons' backyard mud kitchen is made from loose scrap boards on stumps. When we moved to a new house, we filled a box from our actual kitchen of stuff labelled "mud kitchen" like dented pots and extra ladles. Why do we have three colanders? Throw one in the mud kitchen box. We've also got some dump trucks in the mud kitchen area, plus wooden spoons, bowls, and measuring cups. People build them out of pallets. People build them out of plywood. People improvise construction based on their time and materials at hand or look up designs on the internet. A picnic table with pots and pans is fine. Or you could build a whole outside room and call it the mud kitchen. It's all up to the adults to set something up.

Sometimes a mud kitchen might have a water source but that's not really even necessary. It's definitely nice to be able to get some water to add to your creative concoctions but a bucketful from a hose or drinking fountain works just fine. Some mud kitchens keep it dry. Some mud kitchens have no mud! Sand is fine. Dry dirt is fine. Pebbles are fine. Leaves to mix and mash are fine. It's really just about the dedicated space and some kitchen tools to use for mixing, measuring, and mashing.

The children and mud kitchens say yes!

PHOTO BY GAIE JUDSON

PHOTO BY GAIE JUDSON

Bare Feet

Children must to be allowed to be barefoot. They must be allowed to choose. Before there was human history there were children running around barefoot. Little earthlings connected to the earth. Children using their bodies and senses to gather information and feel the planet beneath their feet. How upside down is our world that we would limit something so basic, so human, so fundamentally part of childhood? This could be the ultimate marker of how wacky things had gotten before we all worked together to step back and see the comedy of our errors and collective weird ways and decided to set the stage right again. I can see us all suddenly opening our eyes as if waking from a strange dream, laughing at its absurdity, "we were living in a society—a normal modern one, mind you—except that all of the adults decided that we would force children to wear shoes at all times and never let them take them off. Never let them run free, barefoot. It wasn't punishment, it wasn't to be cruel, it somehow made total sense to us. It just felt normal." This reminds me of dreaming about having three heads and not realizing until later you were dreaming.

For the record: this is not normal thinking. This is backwards, upside-down, and wrong. Yes, there are times when it's too cold to be barefoot. Yes, there are synthetic playground surfacing materials that occasionally get too hot for bare feet. Yes, there may be splintery elements on the play yard that need to be looked after and removed. Yes, muddy bare feet need to be cleaned off. Yes, there could be hazards on your playground that you wouldn't want children stepping on. Yes, there could be a fire drill or an emergency that calls for immediate evacuation and shoe'd children.

These are our responsibilities as adults. It's our job to make the environment safe, think through all the scenarios, and then let the children play. It feels like an insult to our collective adultness to think that we wouldn't be trusted to figure these things out. I'm a bit offended! You should be too. Finding ways to allow children to run barefoot is not rocket science. We have the intelligence and technology to handle it. We can do this. Go ahead and risk-benefit analysis the situation. See how it lines up. Come up with a clear plan for your professional management of bare feet. Write it down. Put it into practice. You can do it.

If the no bare foot rule is a regulatory requirement above your pay-grade, the first step is: double check. Is it really? Look up the regulations and find the wording of that so-called rule. Maybe it is a regulated rule, but maybe it is not. I've heard many times of people thinking they were living under stricter regulations than they actually were. That could be an immediate relief for you and an immediate re-centering of reality. What if there indeed is *not* an anti-barefoot rule, but your regulator calls you out for "child endangerment" when seeing your barefooted children?

Next you could sit them down with your three-ringed binder and walk them through your well-crafted and highly detailed "risk management schemes" for children being barefoot in your yard. That should really do it for a reasonable licensor. But if that doesn't work you always have the right to appeal the report to their supervisor. With your rock-solid risk-benefit analysis, description of your well thought-out safety and emergency backup plans, and your written health and wash-up checklists, you will make it very easy for the supervisor to remove any write-ups, citations, or other such silliness from your inspection record. It's exhausting. It's ridiculous. It feels like a waste of time.

But: these are the times we live in now and it is our job as thoughtful, caring adults to do the tedious work of proving our points to the powers that be, no matter how mindless or backwards it feels. To put the world right-side up we need to move away from the old ways of thinking. *The children can't do it for themselves. They shouldn't have to.* We need to speak up for the children. We need to find the ways to make it right. They have better things to do. Like run around barefoot.

FEET

I show all sorts of wild play images in my presentations—kids with fire, covered in mud, hugging chickens—but often the most controversial… are bare feet!

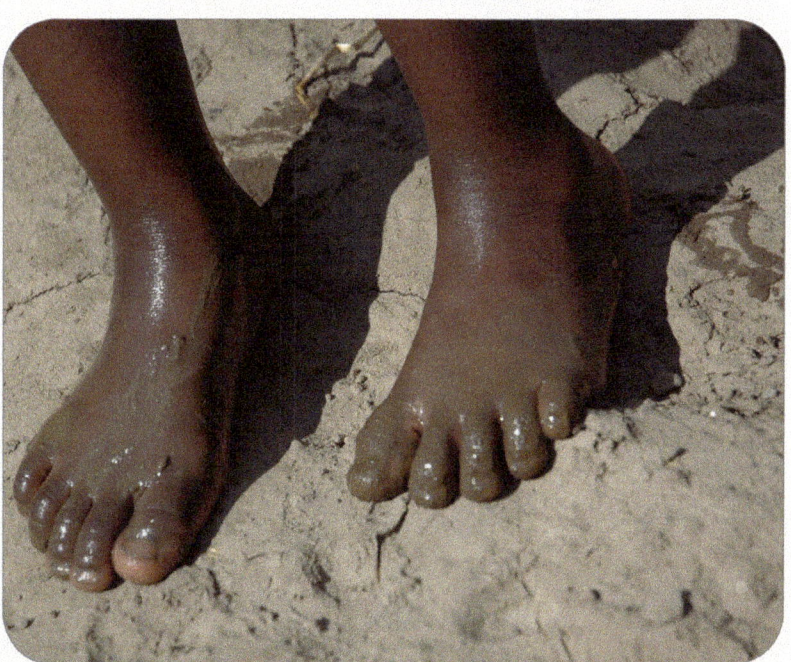

A New Idea

As a designer I love thinking up new ideas for play things—landscapes, products, play features or contraptions. It's exciting to try to come up with something new that sparks children's imaginations and challenges their bodies. Well, I think I have something unique that I'd like to share with you. It's so top secret and brand new that patents aren't even pending yet. I think you'll be interested. Want to hear about it?

The idea is this: a new style of climbing equipment for children of all ages and abilities. This climber is perfect for children just starting to climb as well as those looking for extra challenge and adventure. It's safe, but it's also risky. It easily passes federal playground safety guidelines even as it invites wilder ways of using it.

Some features:

- Comes in a variety of sizes, heights, colors, and degree of challenge.

- Handrail grips for safety and use of upper body strength.

- Can also be used with feet alone to climb.

- Invites fast climbing or slower deliberate climbing.

- Promotes balance and coordination.

- Children are drawn to it immediately and will repeat its challenge over and over in different ways.

- Easily adaptable to any piece of play equipment or as a stand-alone play feature.

- If a child falls while ascending, the climber gently guides them down to where they started in a smooth, safe, gliding motion, until they are ready to make another attempt.

- Provides a quiet space underneath for resting, hiding, or hanging out with friends.

- Makes great sounds when stomped on with feet.

Do you want to see my idea?

Provocatives 129

< gasp! >
IT'S A SLIDE!!

Ok, I'm making a point and I'm making a joke. When I try this gag during talks and presentations the joke completely falls flat as I click the powerpoint slide to reveal my fabulous new invention. I've finally figured out why no one laughs: a lot of people are so aghast at seeing a child climb up a slide and triggered by such a blatant disregard for a time-honored and agreed upon rule passed down from generation to generation that they don't see the humor. Instead, every bell and whistle is going off in their heads. The oft-repeated rule-mantra burned into people's brains "*we climb up the steps, we go down the slide*" takes over and they forget that I was kind of pulling their leg.

During these awkward moments, I'm feeling uncomfortable that no one thought my joke funny and the audiences are uncomfortable because they are seeing one of childhood's 101 commandments being blatantly broken right in front of their eyes. It's actually a comical scene. I've heard gasps and murmurs, seen blank looks then LOTS of talking between audience members and their neighbors.

I've had whole rooms swell with heated talk about the idea of children going up slides—being *allowed* to go up slides. Sanctioned to go up slides?! Encouraged to go up slides?!? *How can that be?* That cannot be! I've spent many breaths of my life telling children not to do this. Well, I never! How do you feel about this?

Who came up with the rule? It's been around long before us. Our generation didn't make it up. But we've somehow adopted it. We now have an opportunity to reclaim the rule and make it our own.

Reclaiming Rules

Why is climbing up slides so appealing to children? Maybe because a child looks at every piece of fixed play equipment as a whole. The whole thing was made for kids and is saying YES: use me, play with me, climb me, slide me. **The child sees possibilities, not limitations.** I learned that my first month as a playground equipment designer when I watched children use a prototype I had spent a long time building. "*Hey, uh, no, um, you're supposed to use this a different way! My idea is for you to use it differently!*" I said to nobody listening as the children used it however they wanted. **My first big lesson as a play designer was that you can never predict how children will use something and you should always design with that fact in mind.** Let things be open-ended and never design them to be only safe if used in a specific way. They're going to be used in whatever ways children feel invited to use them!

I recently was reviewing the United States Consumer Product Safety Commission (CPSC) federal playground safety guidelines and was happily surprised to see their position on children's slide use: "Children can be expected to descend slide chutes in many different positions, rather than always sitting and facing forward as they slide." *Yes!* I thought. *They really get it! They understand children and how they play!* Only to continue reading: "These other positions should be discouraged at all times to minimize injuries." Come on!

They missed that basic design lesson I embarrassingly learned as a 23-year-old novice play designer: that children should be allowed to use play equipment however they want. The guideline-writers understand that they will. I appreciated that fact—they know children! But then to discourage natural, normal uses by children?! That's wrong and upside down. We should be acknowledging the fact that children will come up with multiple uses, celebrate their creativity, and help make it safe for them to do so.

YOU HAVE OPTIONS

- What would happen if you let kids climb up slides?
- What if you did a risk-benefit analysis?
- What if you talked to your colleague-teachers and asked them to look at the benefits?
- What if this was a gateway discussion to other rules you follow?
- What if you all became the new rule makers? According to your culture of play?
- What rules might children come up with for climbing up slides?

MUSINGS ON RULES

To what degree is a rule in place for safety?

How much is it for adults' comfort?

Is it a rule we think we are *supposed* to have?

My son's kindergarten teacher related this experience she had with allowing more play by *not saying no*. She had attended a recent play symposium promoting child-directed play and playworking styles of supporting it. She left thinking, *"Ok, I'll give this a try. I'll see what happens."* So the next week instead of policing the playground and telling every child who wanted to climb up the outside of the climber "no," she decided she wouldn't say anything. She wouldn't say no and she wouldn't say yes and she'd watch what happened as a social experiment. She noticed some children climbed up the outside of the equipment and made it successfully all the way to the top. Other children gave it a try, got maybe halfway up and decided they didn't want to keep going, it wasn't for them, and jumped down. The third group of kids didn't care about climbing the outside at all and didn't attempt it or go near it. The children self-selected. Nobody forced them to do it. Nobody forced them not to do it. The thoughtful adult may have had a tough time at first; who knows how many times she was enforcing that rule during her years as a teacher? But she had the courage to try.

PHOTO BY AMY AHOLA

A school playground is used in a whole different way when school is not in session. There's a breath of fresh air with kids feeling more like kids. I can remember that feeling from my own childhood. A sense of freedom and relief to explore and walk on top of things and do things that would not be allowed during school-sanctioned recess... and yet nobody was getting hurt any more than during recess. Nobody was doing insane things. Nobody wants to go beyond their comfort level too much. The difference between what children will do under our constant policing and control, is actually not that far from what they would do without us there. Slightly more, slightly different. Children want to push the limits - but not THAT far.

WHAT IF?

- How deeply are rules ingrained in our psyches?
- How easily can we switch directions?
- What rule can you question?
- Are there more interesting things you could be saying to children than "no" or "be careful?"
- Are there more creative ways you can use your own time than policing?
- Are there more fun things you could be doing with children?
- What happens when you trust children to know their own limits?
- What percentage of adult-to-child interactions are directive?
- What if we treated children more like equals?
- What if we listened to their thoughts and ideas more?

Provocatives 135

PHOTO BY KISHA REID

Rough and Tumble

Some people think rough and tumble play is the most controversial type of play. But in some ways rough and tumble play isn't controversial at all—because adults simply forbid it and say no! End of story, end of controversy. It makes sense: adults don't want children fighting, bullying, or having physical confrontations. We don't want anyone to get hurt. It's a no-brainer, right?

Except true rough and tumble play is not about any of those things. It's actually about friendship, bonding, touch, togetherness and trust. To the untrained eye play-fighting could appear like real fighting—it involves children "going at it" with each other: wrestling, pushing, squishing or squeezing. That stuff definitely triggers our step in and stop it reflex. Break it up! But by training our eyes to see the difference between aggressive anti-social behavior and playful, pretend anti-social behavior, we can find ways to say yes to this important type of play.

Rough and tumble play comes in all shapes and sizes. It can be play-fighting, wrestling, bumping, chasing, roughhousing, pillow fighting, tickle-monstering, bear hugging, etc. I myself get called in to be the blanketed "brabble brabble monster" at home that attacks and tickles my two young sons. It's exciting and loud with mock aggression, rage and rampage but like any child who likes to roughhouse, I know that it is a subtle operation. A whole set of unspoken rules dictate the play and while it is seemingly wild and crazy it is also completely controlled and able to stop at a moment's notice. I'm pretty good at knowing my own strength and being able to self-regulate during roughhousing. That's one of the big skills it teaches. My older son has finally learned when he plays rough with his younger brother, if he can keep his real strength in check then the play can go on and on. If he takes it too far and really squishes the little guy the fun stops and the game is over. It's a fine line between fun and finished. But those are the lines we want children to learn.

Humans have always been rough and tumbling. Animals play in roughhousing ways too. You've probably seen the videos of young foxes or bear cubs or otters rolling and wrestling and pretending to bite each other. They are practicing their life skills to hunt and protect themselves. But they are also sharing in the joy of being alive with those around them. Children too. Rough and tumble is big body physical play that sharpens coordination, and builds muscles and endurance. It's cognitive play that strategizes and plans moves. It's role-playing and dramatic play that embodies shared stories and heroes' journeys. It teaches self-control, compassion, boundaries, and the difference between right and wrong. Children experience cause and effect as they adjust the play in the moment and see how friends react. They learn conflict resolution, resilience and grit, and how to be flexible and adaptive to the unpredictability of roughhouse play. They learn to read and interpret social cues and know the difference between play-fighting and real aggression. They learn to take turns and cooperate. They learn appropriate uses of strength and power. They learn compassion and forgiveness. They learn how to use their voice and say "Stop!" They even learn how to deal with minor injury or bumps and bruises. With so many positive things about rough and tumble play, why would we ever think of limiting it?

Well, for one thing it can be uncomfortable to see children mock fighting. Our creative accident-imaginers can think of all sorts of negative outcomes. It doesn't take long to fill a page of risks and injuries that could possibly happen as we risk-benefit analyze these situations. But that list of benefits is pretty long too and we know that deep things are happening even as it appears to simply be fun wild play. So, as with all of these risky play activities, with thoughtful management and discussions with children we can devise ways to allow this type of play. Creativity and conversations. Some groups set aside actual spaces for rough and tumble play with soft mats and pillows. Some adults work with the children to come up with rules: "No hitting, no hitting in the face, no hitting below the belt, you can stop the game at any time, only play if it is fun." With our thoughtful care and guidance we can help children to participate and navigate this tricky but fun and beneficial style of risky play.

ROUGH AND TUMBLE: A STORY AND REFLECTION

The group playdate among former preschool friends had wrapped up at Ithaca Children's Garden and my son JJ and his buddy Tao were the last remaining. His mom and I were there too. The boys had been best friends the year before but now were attending separate kindergartens. They are always glad to see each other. At this point in the day they were having fun at the shallow goldfish pond trying to catch fish in pots and pans—sometimes successfully, mostly not, but it didn't matter.

At one point they jumped up from their fishing and chased each other some and ended up in a grassy clear space and without any discussion or verbal communication they started wrestling. One boy grabbed the other and tried to fling him on the ground. It was immediately clear that they were doing this for fun. They were smiling, their eyes were concentrating but joyous, and it was obvious they were enjoying themselves (and obvious they had done this before —probably many times).

Tao's mom and I looked on admiring our boys and getting a kick out of their friendship and play. But we were also watching closely and alertly to see how the rough and tumble was all going. Are they really ok? Everybody cool? And how about the environment around them? Are there any hazards? Any objects they could fall on or hard surfaces, or people that could get in the way? Nope. This is all part of the dynamic risk-benefit analysis. What are benefits of this play? What risks of injury are there? Benefits include the happy reunion of the buddies getting to reconnect and have fun while testing their strength and moves and getting a sweaty good workout. The boys are bonding with each other, feeling that push-pull of friendship trust, even as it appears they are trying to take each other down. Injury risks: well, lots of things could happen—poked eye, twisted arm, bonked head, etc. The list of what-if's could go on and on but so do the benefits and it was clear this play—for now—appeared fine and was nothing we needed to stop. Tao's mom and I were able to relax, commenting how they both seem pretty equally matched. We kept our distance and let the shenanigans continue (while still keeping an eye on things).

The object of the play seemed to grapple, grab, and try to get a good take down. One boy would get a better grip around the neck or waist of the other, spinning, trying to trip or throw back the other while his opponent tried to keep steady or flip the other down. Boom! And laughter, smiles. They would pop right back up again and then race towards each other arms extended grabbing and reaching for a good grip to throw down again.

Then suddenly without a word both boys ran back to the fishing spot to see what the fish were up to. That made me laugh. How did that idea initiate? Who started it? Nobody said anything. It just seemed to spontaneously happen. Ready for a break or release valve I suppose.

Soon enough they were back to the wrestling spot giving it another go. Giving them an opportunity to break it up, Tao's mom asked, "Anyone ready for a snack?" (All adults have their thresholds of seeing children roughhousing, especially their own children!) No takers. The boys definitely heard her—I could see the question registered—but they pretended to ignore her and kept the battle raging. Grabbing, flinging, falling, laughing. Everything was still fine and fun.

But… after a little more time went by I could sense a subtle shift. It was starting to look like not quite as much fun. They were going at it with the same energy but the looks on their faces were changing.

How rough and tumble ends is a big part of the puzzle and why it can be challenging for all of us. *"First comes laughter then comes tears,"* some people say. Roughhousing can end with all parties happy and friendships intact and the bonding is beautiful. But other times it can indeed end in tears. Someone might take it too far, be too rough, or not hear someone saying, "Stop." Someone could get their head actually bonked or feel like someone is being too aggressive or breaking an unspoken rule.

The possibility of physical injury exists, but there is also the possibility of feelings getting hurt, like a friend betraying them by taking it too far. Roughhousing is socially risky. If someone subtly steps over the line it could break trust. And that can hurt too. Also, there can be hurt pride. Who is going to be the one to say, "Let's stop?" That could feel like you losing the game, admitting weakness or vulnerability, giving up. And because that's hard to do, even if both parties might be ready to stop, sometimes rough and tumble play goes further than the players really want.

For adults watching it's always a dance of letting the play go on without our interference. Different ages have different skills and abilities to negotiate a truce. Younger children may need us to check in or ask if everyone is still ok, or actually step in and stop it. I remember other times at my son's preschool when I could sense that the moment for tears was not far away and prepared myself to step in with some adult comment or perspective only to be a moment too late and lines were crossed, feelings hurt, or heads were bonked.

We want our children to have positive experiences. We don't want their feelings or their bodies hurt. And yet, those risky, iffy moments are precisely the moments children need as they learn to navigate life themselves. We can help. We can guide. But for children's long-term health, safety, self-esteem and well-being, it is vital that we let them experience life's tough times as well as good times. That's the full picture. They are going to have to experience life's bumps in the real world. We want them prepared to know how to negotiate with others, know their own limits and judge for themselves what they can and cannot do and what they do and don't want to do. Getting these opportunities in a safe space with you is the best gift you can offer your young people. It's not always pretty and it can sometimes end in tears but these are deep life lessons they are learning that they take with them in their hearts and minds. Yes, it is our job to keep the hazards away, break up any real aggressive violence, guide children as they develop their own coping strategies to deal with these situations, but as much as we can we must let it go. Watch, notice, be alert, read the situation

and subtleties then allow things to happen. Let them be learning opportunities. Your job is mostly not to interfere. Sometimes a subtle remark from the adult is all it takes to help shift or diffuse a situation.

I watched the boys continue their wrestling and saw that faces were tightening and felt like they were getting close to the edge—maybe only seconds away. "You guys ready for a snack?" I quickly asked them again and this time they both immediately said "Yes!" and let go of each other and ran happily to the picnic table to see what the snack was.

That was close. They clearly were ready to stop but not ready to be the ones to say stop. That's my theory anyway. Maybe a moment later one boy would have said let's stop or run back to the fish pond. But one boy also might have thrown down the other in a harder way than would have been fun. Maybe someone was about to get hurt. Both boys were getting tired out and losing some steam and patience.

I don't always get it right as a parent or person practicing playwork strategies, but I have gotten better at letting things go when I can see that the injury risks are low. I love seeing the play unfold. But we don't always get the stopping of play right. **"Least amount of adult intervention as possible" goes the playworker's mantra.** That's my mantra too. I love how in this story the boys were able to stop the play before it went too far. It felt like they made the choice. It wasn't me saying stop or don't do this or don't do that or you guys have had enough. It was more subtle than that. I just gave them an offer to drop the play in a way that had nothing to do with judging the play or the actions of the players or reprimanding someone for taking things too far. It felt like getting an assist in sports—throwing up a lob for a teammate to slam dunk the basketball, passing the hockey puck for another to shoot into the net. I put the offer out there just like Tao's mom had minutes before, but this time they were ready to take it. They were really ready to stop but they needed a tiny bit of help. And the fact that it was me making the snack suggestion helped them "save face." They didn't say they needed to stop. They didn't get hurt or angry or feel weak or beaten. They left the game as equals, without drama. They left as buddies breathing hard and eating snacks.

Some playworking adults might say that I did too much and I should have stayed out completely and let the chips fall where they may and how do children learn if they don't play it out themselves? If there had been no adult around, what would they have done? Did I rob them of an opportunity to grow? Did I adulterate the play? Maybe, or yes, or I'm not sure. It's always good to reflect on the interventions we do into children's play. For a playworker there is no better feeling than getting it "right" and no worse feeling than getting it "wrong." So we reflect and remember for next time.

MIKE HUBER, Early Childhood Education Supervisor
St. David's Center for Child and Family Development
Minnetonka Mills, Minnesota, United States

Author of *Embracing Rough-and-Tumble Play: Teaching with the Body in Mind*

What is rough and tumble play?
Rough and tumble play refers to play that involves the whole body such as running/chase, kicking and throwing balls, climbing, and roughhousing (or wrestling). Often the term is used to refer specifically to roughhousing.

Why is it important for children?
There are a few reasons: It's fun. Children get sensory input that helps them self-regulate. Children with different language abilities can play together as equals. It helps develop the proprioceptive and vestibular senses. It helps build social cohesion among children. It helps children focus on activities after the roughhousing.

What are ways adults can support rough and tumble play?
First, provide a place to engage in R&T safely like a mat.

One adult should be nearby to keep the play safe. Adults can participate. With young children (or children new to R&T), adults can help children learn to read non-verbal cues.

When someone gets hurt, the adult can help children ask, "Are you OK?" and "Can I do anything to help?"

What are some first steps for adults wanting to say "yes" and support some rough and tumble play?
I think pillow fights are a way for many adults to get started because it is boisterous, but there is less body-to-body contact.

Another simple way is to get on your knees, hug the child and then fall down (while still holding them).

Do you have a favorite story of rough and tumble play from a child's perspective?
I had a preschool classroom where all the kids knew each other. One girl joined the class later and was having trouble joining in play. It was the year I introduced roughhousing to my classroom. I started by reading the children a book called *Let's Play Rough* by Lynne Jonelle. It's about a dad wrestling with his kid. After reading it, each child in my class said they wrestle with their dad. The new girl said, "I wrestle with my dad too! I didn't know they wrestled with their dads. Maybe if I wrestle with them, we can be friends." And that is exactly what happened. It turned out, it took two others to push her down.

What's your favorite story of an adult learning to say yes to rough and tumble play?
I did a workshop with my co-hosts from *Teaching with the Body in Mind* podcast about rough and tumble play. There was an older woman who had a family child care program who was very reluctant. She did finally decide that a pillow fight would be fun. She ended up making a pillow for each child. She made a video of group time when she handed each child a pillow. She asked the children what they could do with the pillows. After several ideas (beds for dolls, sleeping on, etc.), she said, "Those are all good ideas. But I was thinking something more like this..." She bopped one of the kids on the head. Within seconds kids were laughing and swinging pillows.

A rough and tumble "aha" moment
After teaching preschool for about 15 years, I had a classroom that was almost completely boys, most of whom needed to move and play physically. I had been able to deal with a handful of children with this need, but not an entire room. I really worked against these children, trying to contain them. I was constantly reminding them not to run, or to keep their hands to themselves. I was getting burnt out and had serious thoughts about finding a different job! Then I decided to learn more about what's behind this need to play rough. I went to see Michelle

Tannock speak about her research on rough-and-tumble play and slowly started to see that I didn't have to learn how to restrict these children to make my job easier. I had to find ways to allow these children to express themselves.

I soon had a mat in my classroom. I also helped the children figure out how to check if it was safe to run in parts of the classroom. (Are there other children or toys that might get run over?) As situations came up, I learned to expand my response and classroom environment to embrace more types of play. My job got easier, but more importantly, more fun. Two years later I had a similar mix of active children (and yes mostly boys), but this time, I had one of my best years teaching. Saying "no" all the time really drains you as a teacher (and as a human being).

Thoughts on risky play
Children need to learn to both assess risk, and take risks that seem manageable. This will look different for different children. Touching a worm may be a risk for one child, while jumping from a boulder may be a risk for another child. In either case, children need to learn that they may get nervous. Their hearts may race, their breath may get short, but they can work through that, and accomplish something.

Rough and tumble play is a perfect way to teach children about consent. Children must ask if they can play rough with another child. The other child must say yes. This is often done with non-verbal cues including soft shoves that become increasingly rough. Children would learn that they still have the right to say stop in the middle of play. Consent is an on-going communication. This is a lesson that can carry over into many areas of adulthood.

Adults can view rough and tumble play as a chance for children to learn how to empathize with others.

Your Own Anarchy Zone

What if you had a corner of your space that was totally dedicated to loose parts, free play and mess? I bet your children would love it. Some preschool teachers recently told me a story about their outdoor play space. Their center was a big believer in messy play with loose parts and natural materials and every day they let the children do whatever they wanted with a huge assortment of materials. But, every day they also worked hard with the children to take everything apart and tidy the space back up. Yes, it's nice to have a clean play yard but it's also nice to have a messy place where anything goes, and can keep going. Just like children in the classroom appreciate when their massive block constructions can stay set up for a couple days to continue the play and invention, children also appreciate being able to have continuity with materials in their outdoor spaces.

One day after cleaning all their hard work constructions up the children asked the teachers, "Can we please have a space that we don't have to clean up—that we can leave messy?" Sometimes we get so ingrained with our routines and mindsets that it takes a childlike perspective to give us pause and reconsider our habits. The open-minded teacher takes a breath and can deeply consider children's ideas and needs—even if they go against ingrained agendas. These were such teachers! Together they thought about the children's request. Hmmm. Could we let them keep a space messy? Not clean up? Really?! The more the teachers thought about it the more they realized the children had a good point: it was kind of silly that the children had to disassemble all the great playstuff they built everyday. Why couldn't they have a space to leave them up?

Well, in this case the playground was a shared space and part of the reason for cleaning the mess was to keep it in ship-shape for other groups that would use it after hours and on weekends. But could there be some other space they could use as a messy "anarchy zone"? Turns out in this story: yes! Believe it or not there was actually a wooded fenced-in space right outside the main playground that nobody used. They had never really looked much at that overgrown space until now. After some good staff conversations, owner permissions, and a Saturday clean-up party they took over the space and gave the children what they wanted: a messy place for loose parts play that could stay messy day after day. Happy ending hooray!

Perhaps you have an undiscovered space outside your fence waiting to become something like this. Even if you don't you could dedicate some of your inside-the-fence playground real estate to a messy loose parts "anarchy zone." The name doesn't matter—call it your S.T.E.M. corner or Outdoor Maker Space. The mission is the same: loose parts + children = possibilities. Like any pile of loose parts, you curate the materials according to your tastes, ideas, and community donations. They could be all natural things like pine cones, pebbles, and tree cookies (slices of tree branches) or a mix of stuff like traffic cones, tennis balls, milk crates and metal spoons. You can let it be a junkyardy mess or still keep it somewhat organized. Nothing wrong with a little tidying up with storage bins and buckets to keep everything in its place. Every mechanic knows that the job is easier when they can find their tools! As with all loose parts play you'll want to keep a good eye out for safety issues like broken materials that need to be discarded as well as watching the general play for any accidents waiting to happen. Your messy space doesn't have to be huge to make a big impression on the play. A mud kitchen could be your ticket. So could a small corner table with sorted loose materials. Maybe you have a whole area dedicated to mixing and making stuff. Or maybe your whole yard is one big messy anarchy zone!

Chickens

Which came first—the chicken or the egg? *You* came first actually, then came your backyard chickens, and then they brought you eggs. Right? No? What?? You don't have chickens!? All of my favorite childcare centers and schools have chickens. They're wacky, they're fun, they eat your leftovers and they give you eggs. And children love them.

With 19 billion chickens estimated living on Earth it's the lucky minority that get to be in a backyard flock with children and adults who love them, name them, and treat them like pets. People all over are adding gardens and composting to their outdoor environments. We love to have children know that their food comes from the earth as they pull carrots out of the ground and nibble on lettuce. Well, how about eggs? Chickens aren't just a pretty face—they produce food for us too. Children love to look for eggs in nests and triumphantly celebrate their discoveries. What better breakfast than farm fresh eggs and veggies from your garden? You might say no, you might laugh it off, but chickens are really quite fun.

It's nice for children to be caretakers once in a while instead of just being the ones cared for. It's nice for children to know that another being depends on them for food and water. It's nice to have another connection with life on our planet. Many chickens love children back and appreciate a good tight hug. They really are entertaining and endlessly fascinating. I've had small backyard flocks of my own and they are a hoot. They have unique personalities and peculiarities that are amusing and memorable. Chicken coop designing is a great project that children can be a part of. Planning, researching and learning about chickens' needs teaches science, construction, and compassion and love for others. True, not every city jurisdiction allows for backyard flocks and licensing might have some thoughts about it. But it *could* work for you and your lucky children. Do a little research and test the waters. Lots of schools and centers have found ways to do it. Yes, it takes a group effort with someone in charge. Chickens don't feed and water themselves, but that's part of their beauty: children can be a part of the timeless tradition of tending to their own animals. Why did the chicken cross the road? To get to her new home in your backyard!

Provocatives 151

CATHERINE MORGAN, Director
The Point Preschool
Sydney, Australia

CHICKEN HOUSE DREAMING

In 2012 we had a dream to make a "forever home" for two chickens. Our dream came from conversations shared and discussed with the children and families. Our connection with the compassionate New South Wales Hen Rescue revealed that many chickens rescued from industrial farms were in need of love and forever homes. In harmony with our commitment to education for sustainability we made the decision to build a home at our place for chickens from donated, recycled and repurposed materials so to also reduce our resource footprint. A waste audit of the food scraps left over from morning tea ("snack" for non-Australians) and lunch and additional food scraps donated by families, revealed there was more than enough to support our three worm farms and left over scraps could be fed to the chickens.

Our journey over the next few years was slow and many times we were faced with obstacles. Sometimes these obstacles seemed insurmountable. Yet we continued to dream.

Over the next three months our children designed the chicken house. They discussed their ideas, drew plans, revised their plans and made their plans come to life using cardboard boxes. These plans and constructions were discussed again and continued to be altered many times. Finally after much shared decision-making and collaboration, a final design was choosen by the children.

Our journey was a journey of engagement, collaboration and reciprocity with the children, educators, families, neighbours, friends, the community, and the Sutherland Shire Council.

Our children and families, with Phil as our mentor, collaborated to build the construction. Our children continued to demonstrate their competency and dedication to the project. We were a group with a common goal and a very strong sense of connection to build the best chicken house that would keep our chickens safe and also be a place of beauty.

Together we were decision makers, creative problem solvers, imaginative designers, courageous advocates and most importantly, nurturing, respectful and loving citizens.

Our chicken house took over 2.5 years to complete which was very significant to our journey. The extended length of time fostered greater engagement and collaboration with the project and most importantly, engagement and connection with each other.

During the project, many families were inspired to build their own chicken houses from repurposed materials and

welcome chickens into their lives. This supported our goal, to not only reduce our resource footprint but to positively influence our families and wider community to also reduce their resource footprint and open their hearts to chickens.

Our chickens give us the gift of their delicious eggs. Our children have learned where food comes from and about "food miles." We have reduced our reliance on transportation to deliver eggs, reducing our food miles and carbon emissions. We learned that chicken manure is amazing for gardens. We learned what food chickens eat and how to more effectively sort our food scraps for the worms, compost and chickens. We learned about landfill and waste management and have reduced our landfill waste. Our project empowered our children to be active decision makers and advocates to embedding more sustainable practices into our lives and the lives of families and the community. We learned to care for our chickens.

And most importantly, we have experienced the great joy and delight our chickens have brought to our lives. We didn't realize how much we would fall in love with our chickens and how our chicken house project would deepen our children's, families' and community's sense of belonging and connection to place.

Our children excitedly arrive at preschool each day with food scraps from home to give to our beautiful chickens. They sort their scraps from their morning tea and lunch and give these to "the girls." They feed the chickens and provide them with water every day and delight in collecting their eggs. Our children often sit and watch and talk to our girls. We love hearing their caring conversations and their laughter when the girls run over to the fence in anticipation of being fed. The children remind us on Mondays and Fridays that we need to complete our jobs to make the girls' home beautiful. The children help rake, shovel and sweep. They place new straw in the girls' nesting boxes and around their house. And they water the flowers in the planter boxes attached to the chicken

house and the lavender, mint and rosemary growing in their garden. During our 12-week preschool holiday, our children delight in visiting the school to care for the chickens.

When I think back to the day we first talked about the idea of having chickens come to live with us at preschool, I know what we were really saying was we had room in our hearts to love chickens. This realization fills me with an overwhelming sense of joy. And this is what our chickens bring to us—love, joy and wonder. I didn't know we could all love chickens so much. And our lives are richer with the girls sharing our place with us.

PHOTOS COURTESY OF THE POINT PRESCHOOL

PHOTO BY SARA GILLIAM

Mixed-Age

What if the members of your family couldn't be together because you were different ages? That would be weird! Unthinkable! Outrageous! But, we do that with children everyday in schools and childcare centers. We segregate them according to their ages and rules dissuade us from letting different age groups mingle even though we know it's beneficial.

Who made this rule up way back when? Was it for health and safety reasons? Did they mistakenly think that all children develop at the same rate based on the calendar? Was it easier to organize and statistically more efficient to catalogue children this way? Or maybe when they did their initial risk-benefit analyses on mixed-age groupings they forget to include the benefits—that must be it!

We now know that mixing the ages has so many benefits for all the ages involved. If you only were concerned with protecting little kids from big kids, age segregation would make a lot of sense. If you took out the factor that thoughtful, caring, professional adults are present in the mix too, maybe age segregation would make sense.

But if you think about family life, neighborhood life, and the general world around us, everything else is a mixed-age environment. Young people and old people. Aunts and uncles. Brothers and sisters and cousins. It's all perfectly normal and a natural way of being. So why in the world would we limit ourselves and our children from experiencing the love, connections, human bonding and learning that comes from being with others of a variety of ages?

Ask most family child care professionals and they'll tell you that multi-age bonding is one of their favorite aspects of their daily work life. "I have five children ages six-months through 11-years-old. Everybody gets along so well! The younger ones learn from the older ones. The older children get to be nurturers and caretakers. They are my big helpers with the babies." Ask a large childcare center director who bends the rules of age segregation and they'll tell you they are standing up for something fundamental to the rights of children. "Children need to be with children of different ages. It's not healthy for children to only mingle with children their exact age! It takes away so much learning that happens when younger children can see what the older children are doing. Children who have bigger brothers and sisters at home come in having way more skills and tricks than children who don't. And children who have younger siblings are automatically more nurturing and compassionate with younger schoolmates."

We want all children to have those opportunities to be both teacher and learner. **All wisdom does not have to come from the adults in the room.** Babies and toddlers have a natural attraction to older children and want to see what they are up to. School age situations are the very same way. Many private school philosophies group multi-age children in their classrooms. They know the benefits and necessity. Montessori and Waldorf schools have this as a fundamental part of their schooling philosophies. Public schools get a flavor for this when ages overlap on the playground at recess.

PHOTO BY AMY AHOLA

PHOTO BY AMY AHOLA

Sometimes it is important to have age groups separated. Big bodies can move faster and more wildly than small ones. Nobody wants bigger kids crashing through wobbling toddlers or stepping on sleeping babies. But don't you think there could be a way that mindful adults could manage a mixing like that? Yes! Another factor keeping the ages apart is the design of fixed playground equipment. While natural playscapes with hills, sand, paths, and trees invite children of all ages to safety explore in a multitude of ways, fixed play equipment is geared for specifically-sized children and children with similar physical abilities. There are definitely school-age pieces of equipment that you wouldn't want toddlers exploring! That can indeed be dangerous, especially for adventurous babies and toddlers who are hardwired to push limits. The triple spiral slide is not for you Susie! Please stay off the giant metal climber Jimmy!

Once your environment is safe for mixed-ages then we can get to the good stuff: the magic and beauty of the human connections when we blend children together. Hearts can open when bigger kids get to be nurturers of younger ones and younger children get to look up to the big ones. It sparks ideas, it radiates love, it offers the chance for a school or center to inch its way closer to family. "Kids are pack animals" a neighbor with 5 children once remarked to me as we watched his kids run through a meadow on his farm. The old ones take care of the young ones. The young ones follow the old ones. There are

A lot of these issues could be solved through intelligent design. We could design our environments to be suited for all ages. That's one of the beautiful things about going to the beach—it's great for all ages, right? Babies get a sensory experience, toddlers dig and pour, preschoolers build castles, collect shells and dig holes, and older children with bigger shovels and buckets can make elaborate sand creations and constructions. The same could go for your yard with a hill and playhouses, grass and a shed full of loose parts. You're wise enough to manage the stuff. You can help big kids watch out for the little ones. You can also include "baby corrals" in your design that can keep the little ones extra safe when the wild things start happening in bigger parts of your yard. There are a million solutions you can devise to conquer the issue of age-segregated design. I know you can do it.

times when the little ones want to stretch their abilities and try what the big ones are doing. But there are also times when older children want to step back and play like younger children. They need that too! And it could feel weird or embarrassing to want to play small when you are only surrounded by like-aged peers. But it doesn't feel silly when you're playing with littler people. Even 8-year-olds have younger "inner children" that want to play with playdoh and puppets! (I can tell our teenage babysitter really enjoys playing with blocks, trains, and magnetic tiles with my young sons—it might feel funny trying to do that just with other middle schoolers!) So if our goal is to provide the most beautiful, varied, supportive environments for our children, let's not forget to include a most important piece—children of all ages and abilities.

DEB THOMPSON,
Manager of Children's Programs and Child Care Services
The University of British Columbia (UBC)
Vancouver, BC, Canada

*UBC Child Care Services includes over 31 different licensed childcare programs serving families with children in infancy through 12 years old with both **typical-age** classrooms and **mixed-age** classrooms. Because Deb oversees both scenarios and because she researched mixed-age programs for her doctorate, I thought she would be a great person to shed some light on the subject.*

Why is mixed-age so special? What are the benefits?
I would not describe mixed-age as so special but rather as another way of doing child care, one that invites us to challenge unexamined assumptions about children and age.

Having a wide child age range in a child care centre offers resistance to the normalization that age segregation sometimes produces. For example, younger children have opportunities to do big kid things like climb challenging structures while older children have opportunities to perhaps follow a unique developmental course. In addition, mixed-age centres offer the potential of reducing the number of child care environments that a child experiences. That can help a child develop lasting relationships with both other children and adult caregivers.

Families may benefit when siblings can be together. Children without siblings experience an environment that includes younger and/or older children, in other words, an environment similar to a family. Fewer childcare arrangements can offer families stability.

Why is mixed-age not typical?
I think that mixed-age is not typical in licensed child care because it is often not permitted by regulations. It is very typical in most other life situations: communities, neighborhoods and families.

I believe the regulations have emerged in response to **developmentalism**, which refers to the application of child development theory and knowledge to child-rearing in general and to child care centres and other early childhood education settings in particular. Developmental theory described through age norms is so entwined with our understandings about children and about best practices that it can be hard to think about children or early years practices without age-based assumptions. The premise that age predicts development leads logically to the conclusion that developmentally appropriate practices can be determined by child age. It becomes easy to believe we know who children are, and what best practices are, based on child age. It can seem natural and right to apply age-predicted developmental theory to early years practices and to group children by age. We establish the desired development outcomes for a particular-aged child through reference to their age as a shorthand for development and then we plan and implement environments that support those outcomes. Child age then determines the optimal physical and social child care environments. Structural standards about what environments for particular-aged children emerge leading to rules and regulations about what is required for children based on their age. However, this logic fails when other factors besides age are considered to be important in human development. Mixed-age groupings work to disrupt developmental assumptions about children based on age.

How can you set it up for success?
This is a very important question but does not have an easy answer. Of course, it depends what is meant by success. What mixing age groups cannot do is offer less expensive child care. If the goal is to reduce cost, a mixed-age project will either fail outright or will succeed financially but provide an environment that fails children.

Our mixed-age centres operate with the same adult/child ratios that our age segregated centres do and ratios are the most significant factor in cost. So for example the smallest grouping in our mixed-age centres includes one adult, four children over three years of age and two children under three years of age. The comparable groupings in the segregated centres would be one adult for eight children over three and one adult for four children under three. The cost (and therefore fee) is the same as in our other centres.

Mixed-age grouping requires flexible, individualized, responsive pedagogical practices. Challenging developmental theory as the one and only truth about children does not mean that we can disregard developmental differences or ignore that age often does correlate with development. A pedagogy that both challenges and accepts developmentalism demands, means that the early childhood educators working with a mixed-age group must be highly self-reflective, critical thinkers who are flexible, thoughtful and base their practice on listening carefully to children. In other words, they must be extremely skilled.

In addition, the places and spaces of mixed-age centres need to be adaptable and carefully planned. The wide age range means that the range of risk and challenge must be greater. All spaces for children need to provide both risk and challenge for them and also coaching about risk and challenge assessment—in other words, freedom and supervision. A mixed-age grouping increases the challenge for the early childhood educator. Success will rest on the pedagogical beliefs and practices of the adults and the support they receive.

What are challenges?
The challenges lie in the increased complexity that a wide range of development produces. Children will not necessarily fit easily into a planned schedule and many things, such as group time, diaper changes, snacks will have to happen simultaneously. The need for flexibility is great. There is more likelihood that one child—probably young—will disrupt the complicated play of others—who may be older. For example a curious toddler may take a block that looks interesting for a ride in a small wagon; however, said block had been the cornerstone of a structure created by other children that is now destroyed.

What do you appreciate about mixed-age settings?
I like the sense of community that is created. I like the opportunity for siblings to be together. I love the opportunity to think differently about children, pedagogy and relationships that it produces.

We created our centres beyond what regulations demand. We have large centres that are well equipped; we have beautiful natural playgrounds with built-in challenge; we have a large organization that supports us; we researched our practice and continue to engage in discussion and reflection. And finally, we hired and continue to hire educated, licensed, reflective, thoughtful, responsive educators to work in the centres and we provide them support as they confront the challenges the model produces. There can be no question that it is a challenging structure that involves hard work and commitment on the part of the educators. Finally, it is also important to work closely with the licensing agency as they provide us with guidance.

PHOTO COURTESY OF UBC CHILD CARE SERVICES

AMY AHOLA, Owner/Operator/Primary Caregiver
Child Central Station Group Home Daycare
Marquette, Michigan, United States

I run a mixed-age program in Michigan. We are licensed for children from birth to age 12. I don't think I have ever had an infant younger than 6 weeks, but we always have a wide mix of children in the bunch. In addition to our home-based program, I travel and speak at various early childhood conferences. One of the biggest questions I get is, what do you do with the infants and toddlers? The answer is simple: the children are all part of our program, and the infants and toddlers participate in every aspect of our program. Older children learn to trust themselves and to be mindful of younger children. Younger children thrive when they mimic and play side-by-side with the older children.

A couple of years ago, my licensing consultant and the head of licensing in our state stopped by for my interim inspection. When they arrived we were inside, but we were on our way out, so they followed us outside. The children were of course a bit distracted by the fact that we had guests and were testing boundaries a bit more than usual (which is pretty standard and to be expected). The older children found one of the largest ropes that they could find in the back yard and proceeded to have a giant game of running tug-of-war. The rope was probably about 15-20' feet long. I like to give children longer lengths of rope for a variety of reasons, the biggest being that you can't do a whole lot with short pieces of rope. If all the children want to play with it, you need a long piece, and if you are going to tie up a bunch of things, you need a long rope!

The children were running and tugging, and running and tugging and they almost clothes-lined a young toddler. Notice, I said ALMOST. This brought up a discussion and some concerns from my consultant. She asked me, "Tell me about the rope." I of course shared much of what I mentioned here to you…short ropes can't be used for much, longer ropes are needed for most of the things children need rope for. She mentioned that the children had "almost" knocked over the younger child and I quickly noted, yes ALMOST, but they didn't.

They didn't knock that child over because they have had a lot of practice playing with and near young children. They know that in order to be a part of our family home program we need to find ways to make sure that all of the children's needs are met, and that they can run and play rough, but they need to be aware of their surroundings. Now, this doesn't mean to run off and give every child in a mixed-aged program 20 feet of rope and they will avoid the younger children when they run with it…because that doesn't always happen, but it is a prime example of children being able to manage risk and their surroundings when they are given opportunities to do so.

It also doesn't mean that you can just allow children opportunities to take risks without making sure to have very present and attentive adults. The more opportunities you provide for risk-taking, the more you need to make sure that you or other adults can be there to help be guardrails when necessary. Primarily for mobile infants and younger toddlers who are ready to follow the big kids, but don't quite have the skills and development to understand their own limitations. I find the same to be true when we start to look at materials. I know a lot of programs limit some of the materials used because of having younger children present. We have to worry about this too, but instead of eliminating materials, we make sure that younger children have extra support when using materials that may be smaller than their mouths, that they could choke on. We still allow them to explore those materials, but only when we are present.

When something challenges me with the children or an activity, I always try to get to the root of why it bothers/challenges me. I try to see if I have concerns about what the child is trying to tell me that they need. If I am unable to say yes to that activity as it is being presented to me, I try to figure out how else can I meet that need. I can't let a child hit another child to harm them, but I can let them wrestle... I can give the child other things to hit.

Bringing babies outside??? In the winter? In the snow? How do you do that?

I get these questions a lot...

The simple answer is.... We bring the babies with us! Sometimes, babies cry. They cry to communicate because they cannot talk. Being outside as an infant in our cold

PHOTO BY AMY AHOLA

weather can sometimes be a challenge, and younger toddlers often have a hard time adjusting to the winter gear they have to wear as well. We try to help the younger children adjust by bringing snow inside and exploring it without all of our extra gear.

The other piece is our own attitudes and excitement about winter weather. If we are not excited about playing in the snow, young children pick up on that! Sometimes, I will put a plastic swimming pool outside to put infants in to give them a different surface to be on than the snow. It is a transition piece; I also have some outdoor blankets (from Tuffo) that work great as an extra barrier until the younger children are more comfortable with venturing into the fluffy white stuff. We also have some infant sleds… but in all seriousness, most children do not need that long of a transition period, and some of the children love taking snowbank naps.

All of the children are given the opportunity to play in all types of weather!

PHOTO BY AMY AHOLA

PHOTO COURTESY OF TAKOMA PARK COOP

Sticks

We all love having trees in our outdoor spaces. Trees provide shade, blow in the wind, create a canopy ceiling, drop leaves, create seasonal interest, and can be homes for birds, bugs and other animals. Trees give good hugs and like many plants in the playground they also provide wonderful loose materials for children's play like leaves, nuts, berries, fruit, bark…and sticks!

Gasp! Sticks! Oh yes, they could poke your eye out but they can also do a million other things in the hands of creative children. Sticks offer them the means to make believe. Sticks can be used for stirring soups, stews, and poisons. They can be digging implements in sand pits and dirt piles. Sticks can be flag poles and raw materials for building forts, dens, and hideouts. Sticks can be pretend musical instruments, and they can be staffs for walking. They can line the floor plan of a fancy house or mark the grave of a dead bird. You can limbo dance under a stick and you can build a bridge with sticks. You can point with a stick and scratch works of art in the ground with a stick. Sticks can become sculpture or painted works of art. Mobiles can be built from a couple good sticks, string, and other stuff you find. Sticks can be sports equipment to hit hockey pucks and tennis balls. Sticks can be used to pry up rocks to look for bugs. Sticks make good snowmen arms. Sticks can be fairy princess magical wands. I've had many a spell come my way through the end of a wizarding stick-wand. Wizards also need sticks to ride on as do cowboys, police officers, witches and space aliens. Did you know that sticks are good protection against zombies?

In 2008 the stick finally got the recognition it deserves and was inducted into the National Toy Hall of Fame by the Strong National Museum of Play. Congratulations stick! But even with such accolades and praise the stick often gets a bad rap. The poor stick may be one of the loose play parts that makes adults the most nervous. It's true that you don't want to be on the wrong end of a swatting stick and that sticks can be used as weapons as readily as they may be used as sculpture.

But couldn't that risky play be managed with a few thoughtful rules or guidelines? No hitting people with sticks is pretty straight-forward and probably would get the support of children. No running with sticks or no raising sticks above your head are all simple rules that could keep children safer and help adults feel more comfortable with the use of these award-winning play elements.

Many adults get nervous around sticks. We are good at imagining the worst thing that could happen. A toddler picks up a stick and our inner protector alarms go off ding ding ding: stick in the mouth, stick in the eye, stick in a friend's eye. *Drop that stick Ginny. We don't play with sticks Billy. What you find on the ground, stays on the ground.* It must be a bit puzzling for children to see adults reacting so nervously about something so simple as a stick. *Do sticks want to jump out and hurt us? Are they dangerous? They seem like, well, sticks. Should I be scared of sticks? My teachers seem scared. Now they are scaring me!* We're probably not scared of sticks but more about what a stick in the wrong hands could do. Are children's hands the wrong hands? I guess they could be. It's true that children are not always aware of their surroundings

PHOTO COURTESY OF TAKOMA PARK COOP

PHOTO BY KISHA REID

moment of anger, or imagination? Is the child looking for a tool for their play? Or just exploring their surroundings? Is that infant about to bite on that stick? Probably. If you watch you'll know right away. And because you know your children and what they might get up to at any given moment, you should be able to predict the direction the stick play may take based on your knowledge of past experiences.

Then as you watch the play develop you can ponder the benefits and the imaginative things a child can create and discover with that simple stick. Do the benefits outweigh the risks? Can you trust that your straight-forward rules will manage mishaps? Can you find new ways to say yes to the award-winning stick?

and could whap a stick against an unsuspecting friend or an unsuspecting friend could absent-mindedly stumble into the wild stick waving of others.

But the same goes with everything children use in the classroom or on the playground. They have to practice being mindful of themselves and others. (I certainly try to keep a stick length's away from a stick-wielding child. It's a good skill to learn!) Another good skill to learn and practice as adults is to take a moment when we see something that triggers us, like a child with a stick, and before we say *no*, first watch what is happening. Like learning to read children's rough and tumble facial expressions we can also learn to read a child's stick skills and intentions. What does it look like they are about to do with that stick? Go on a rampage? Or are they just inspecting it? It's pretty easy to tell the difference if you take that moment to watch. What is the context of the stick being picked up? Is it in a

PHOTO COURTESY OF TAKOMA PARK COOP

Tree Climbing

As long as there have been trees and children there have been children climbing trees. We humans have a natural desire to go up, up, up and take things to the next level. That is the goal of childhood development, and in physical terms trees literally scaffold children up and offer them choices and challenges beyond what they have done before. It's a metaphor for life, this climbing of trees.

First it takes guts and skills to even get started. Getting yourself in the game, up in the tree, can sometimes be the trickiest part. *How do we get in this thing? How do we get started?* For many early childhood professionals who allow tree climbing this is the first rule: *you have to be able to get in the tree yourself.* If you can negotiate your way up and in then you probably can succeed in the branches above. But if a child can't get themselves into the tree then they may not be ready to be safe higher up. Tree climbing takes skill, awareness, and deliberate decision-making. A child has to learn to trust themselves as well as trust the tree. They have to learn to read the tree. Which branches are safe and which are not? Which branches are alive and which are not? Which branches can hold their weight and which branches cannot? Which ones are within safe reach and which ones feel more dangerous? Tree climbing provides deep, real-life risk-assessment opportunities as children carefully navigate their way through it. Standardized fixed playground equipment can provide a little bit of these challenges (let's face it, the best play equipment is really just trying to be a tree) but they don't come close to offering the level of challenge, risk, unevenness, organic-ness, uncertainty, thrill, awe and respect that climbing a living tree provides.

But it's not for the faint of heart. Falling out of a tree is no joke. It has clear dangers and a chance of failure. Mistakes can happen and a climber could get hurt in a fall. Even badly hurt. It's obvious why adults often don't let children climb trees. When we look at the tree climbing risk on a scale of how bad the injuries might be depending on the tree and the child, a tree fall could be bad. That alone is a good reason to not let children climb. As a play designer, supporter, and risk-benefit analyzer I myself draw the lines at head injury, long bone breakages, and puncture wounds. Yuck. A bad fall from high in a tree could cause all these injuries at once! Why are we even talking about this?!?!

Well, we're talking about it because there are benefits and opportunities with tree climbing that children cannot get anywhere else.

The climber knows there are real dangers. The blood gets pumping not only for the adults watching but for the climbers themselves. The higher they go the more dangerous it is to fall, so the more they need to make sure they don't fall! Is it ok to literally put a child's health and

safety in their own hands? Is it right to trust them with themselves? A tree makes us ask these questions.

I remember climbing a giant pine tree as a boy that had very regularly-spaced branches that let you climb quite high off the ground. The branches were strong and the climbing fairly easy but the view from the top put me into some early existential ponderings about the nature of life and death. Looking down at the sidewalk and ground below me I could easily contemplate what would happen if I slipped and fell. It wouldn't be good. I'd heard stories about kids falling out of trees and breaking their arms. If I misstepped, miscalculated, or a branch I thought was safe wasn't, then I had a long way down to fall. Could I die? Could I break my leg or arm or neck? Yes, actually. That stark obvious realization made me grip the branches tighter, plan my descent more carefully, and make my way down more deliberately. I made it down safely and felt much relief standing on the firm ground. I never climbed that tree again though I've climbed plenty more since then. But what struck me, even as a child, was a feeling that my own life was in my own hands.

As we get older and come of age our lives are indeed in our own hands. We grow up and are responsible for ourselves. But when do we get to practice this skill of self-responsibility? How do we gain the ability to focus,

assess, plan, practice, decide, be mindful, be deliberate, be aware? Climbing trees isn't the only way to practice these skills but it certainly offers up many lessons about ourselves, our limits, and our tolerance for risk.

One of those lessons has to do with the connection between living child and living tree that goes back before the beginning of time. As humans, our primate cousins have all lived and played in the trees. Monkeys, Apes, Orangutans, and Chimpanzees all have specialized hands to grip tree branches. Opposable thumbs! Look at your hands: very similar to a monkey's. (But much nicer-looking.) Could it be that before our fingers typed on computers, texted on phones, and held books in our grip that our hands were made to grasp branches? Could it be that in our DNA we have a natural connection to the trees? I think so, on many levels. Like many things in our world, children display humanity's inner connections to the planet more clearly than we adults do. Yes, climbing trees could simply be a fun and thrilling activity to partake in. But, it could also be hardwired in the human brain as a defense mechanism from danger. Like children being drawn to small hidey places, they also seem drawn to climb up and away from trouble on the ground. Built-in survival mechanisms. So they practice, and get better and more confident and skilled. In our modern age we might not need the physical tree-climbing skills to survive in the jungles or deep woods, but the act of learning to successfully climb gives us another set of skills that lead to our survival and adaptation to life.

It's that "learning to assess risks by themselves" subject again. We adults need to do our part to protect our young, but at some point they need to be able to protect themselves from danger and risky situations. Every tree branch tried gives children a window into their soul and an understanding of what they feel comfortable with and what they don't. Choices. We want children to have choices in how they can play but we also want them to learn to make healthy choices to keep themselves safe in real world situations. The choices could come through

TREE CLIMBING SAFETY IDEAS

In order to say yes to tree climbing, some groups treat the tree like a piece of fixed play equipment and put down soft fall material under the tree that meets playground safety guidelines. Some groups decide with children what branches are safe and what is the height limit to climbing and place markers on branches to show which branches are the limit. Some groups trim all pokey branches from a tree climbing tree. Other groups require children take off their shoes before they climb a tree, to have the best grip possible!

discussions on the ground about safety and hazards associated with tree climbing—someone needs to teach them about how to climb and what to look out for. But the real choices come up in the tree, away from the adults, out of reach but still within earshot.

That might be what makes us nervous and afraid—we are giving control over to the children themselves. We are left behind on the ground while they reach for what's next on their upward journeys. As in life we can only hope that we gave them enough encouragement and instruction, and taught them to think for themselves—to be able to handle themselves in a tricky situation. We're helpless as they grow beyond our control. It becomes up to them to live their lives. The best we can do is help them learn to navigate risks and be a supportive presence as they climb the tree of life.

Tools

We can give children cheap plastic pretend tools and that's ok for certain young toddlers I suppose. But at some point it's time to let children do projects using real life tools of the trades. Of course children should be taught about tool safety and hazards. Tools aren't toys to mess around with. But with proper safety instructions, rules, and guidelines most children can absolutely be trusted to use tools like saws, drills, hammers, wrenches, screwdrivers, knives, scissors, and gas welders. Ok, I'm kidding about the welders but not about the other tools.

Sometimes the tools are there to work on projects, but more often than not, especially for preschoolers, the project is simply: using the tool. Remember how in the 1970's and 1980's every classroom would have a stump pounded with nails and hammers? Well, those stumps still exist and right this minute there are preschool children all over the world with safety goggles happily and carefully pounding nails into stumps. Schools are setting up "maker spaces" with tools to help their makings. "Carpentry corners" are filled with scrap boards and tools to cut them and fasten them together. Like so many aspects of the adult world, children are drawn to authentic adult tools. They want to drill. They want to saw. They want to glue and hammer and bolt. Could you have a space dedicated to safe tool use? Could you set up a woodshop, workshop,

Provocatives 175

PHOTO COURTESY OF TAKOMA PARK COOP

PHOTO COURTESY OF TAKOMA PARK COOP

or tool area? How could you start? How would you talk to your children about tool use? Could you bring in a tool expert parent to show your class the ropes?

I wouldn't let saws be dangling just anywhere and all of this stuff should be used with utmost care and close adult supervision. I wouldn't think of tool use exactly as play and wouldn't suggest you have tools at the ready for anything-goes unsupervised adventures. (Again, I have my limits.) It is also good to consider purchasing tools that are sized for children. We definitely want children to be

able to use "real" (not toy) tools, but it is safer to have tools sized to fit their hands and bodies.

It is important that we respect children's ability to learn safety rules, honor their interest in using real tools from the adult world, and trust them to be able to use them in safe, responsible ways. Every child is different and some tools can be dangerous in the wrong hands but with proper supervision and guidance every child can have the opportunity to try their hands at real-world tool use.

Licensing Perspective 1

JIM MURPHY, Executive Director
The National Association for Regulatory Administration
(NARA)

What is the goal of licensing / accreditation?
The goal of licensing in child care is to ensure the health and safety of children and youth in care in regulated environments, such as foster homes, child care facilities, and family child care homes. It includes a process of reviewing the program relative to state/provincial regulations to ensure compliance of health and safety expectations for operating the program.

Accreditation is different than licensing, and in some cases the standards may exceed the expectation of the related regulation in licensing. Often times accreditation is voluntary, and includes a third-party review of the program environment and services based on the accreditation standards. Most accreditation standards use licensing standards as the foundation and then build upon it.

What are the thoughts about risk and risky play?
Risk is essential for the positive development of children. Children need to be exposed to a safe level of risk so they can understand how to assess situations in the real world. They need to understand the pros and cons of accepting risk, as well as how to identify and manage risk in their play.

How has the view of risk and risky play evolved?
It has ebbed and flowed as parenting styles have done the same. During periods of hyper vigilance, we tend to reduce the amount of risk children are exposed to. We are moving back into a time where individuals see the function and benefits of risk in children's development.

What should the role of regulators and risk be?
Regulators should take an objective view of the activity/proposed activity, as well as the intent of the related regulation(s), with the ultimate goals of safety and protection, while supporting a wide range of appropriate activities and learning experiences. Discussion and understanding of the risk assessment and management process by the provider can assist in this understanding as well. *At the most fundamental core, regulators and providers need to work together to ensure situations that pose risk to children are intentional and not a result of minimum supervision or negligence.*

Where would you like to see the thinking and practice go regarding risky play?
From a regulatory perspective, we would like to see deeper thought, planning, and management of risk-related to play and activities. Having a well thought out plan that minimizes risk, without always needing to eliminate all risk can maximize the scope and breadth of activities the children and youth can experience. Emphasis is needed on the intentional planning of risky play in care environments. The lack of planning and pre-planning analysis and action is what can, at times, lead to unnecessary injury, up to and including the potential of death.

Advice for providers wanting to allow for more risky play?

- Planning should be thoughtful, intentional, and not rushed.

- Important to communicate expectations with teachers.

- Communicate with the families so there is an understanding of what is happening.

- Have a well thought out plan that demonstrates that risks were identified and assessed, and that measures are in place to minimize risk, while providing adequate supervision throughout the activity.

- Show alignment between the risky play and the regulations so it is clear there is an intentional plan.

How to best talk to your licensor about this stuff?
Open and honest communication works the best. Regulators are not the enemy and are not out there simply trying to close programs down, and there is no quota for having to cite programs on non-compliance. Regulators simply want to protect the health and safety of children in care, and the easiest way is when they are able to work closely with providers and observe providers being mindful and deliberate regarding activities, especially when they involve risk. The greater the potential risk—the greater the planning should be.

Advice for licensors who are coming into contact with groups doing mindful risky play?
Be open minded while assessing activities relative to the intent of regulations. Talk with staff to understand their thought process and risk assessment and mitigation process they used, as well as what additional measures may have been put in place to ensure the health and welfare of the children and youth.

How can providers and licensors best work together on these issues?

- Ask lots of questions and actively listen to the answers.

- Providers and licensors should work together through the planning process.

What does an ideal play space look like?

- Lots of different materials for the children to interact with.

- Equipment that promotes gross motor skills.

- Open ended materials for exploration and discovery.

- Time for the children to freely interact in the environment.

What else would you want providers to know?
When a particularly risky activity is being considered, engage regulators early in the process to help determine the appropriateness, as well as possible safety measures to employ, for the activity. Regulators are your partners in this process. Avoid surprises and embrace their role in working with you to ensure the health and safety for both children and youth as well as the staff.

Partner with the providers and continue to create opportunities to work together rather than the perception of working against each other. We are all aiming for the same goal for the children and youth, and cooperation is the best way to achieve that end.

How to best show licensors that you are being mindful and thoughtful, even if you are allowing more risks?
Plans, ideas, and activities need to be well thought out with related regulations identified and potential risks addressed. Having a written outline of the process that was used, with the related regulations identified, along with associated measures to ensure the participants health and safety, would show thoughtfulness and planning.

Licensing Perspective 2

ALIZA YAIR, Outdoor Preschool Pilot Program Specialist
DEBBIE GROFF, Outdoor Preschool Pilot Project Manager
Washington State Department of Children, Youth, and Families

What is the importance of managing risky play for healthy child development?
Research shows that some elements of challenge and risk are necessary for children's optimal physical, emotional, and cognitive development. Children are also active learners, who learn and grow through play and exploration. Yet they are also learning about consequences, and so it is the role of adults to create spaces and conditions that support their exploration, but also ensure their safety.

With regards to risky play, where the risk of injury is more pronounced than in other types of play, teachers can and should remove or make inaccessible the hazards that children can't manage themselves. With the hazards out of the way, teachers can then also provide the safety net of their presence, guidance, and potential intervention during risky play activities that are developmentally appropriate for the child. By doing this, the teacher can create a program where children can engage in those necessary zones of development, trying something new and brave, but without truly exposing the child to danger beyond what they can manage physically, emotionally, or mentally.

In Washington, we are starting to develop our state systems for supporting risky play through our Outdoor Preschool Pilot, a project to develop licensing standards for outdoor, nature-based early learning programs. Because these programs take place in nature, we cannot apply the traditional playground safety standards for the areas where children will play. So what does safety look like then? Based on the advice and feedback of our pilot programs, we are figuring out how to support a process-based approach to safety, including the importance of creating informed benefit-risk assessments, training staff on these standards for policies and procedures, as well as identifying and addressing teachers' training needs.

When people want to provide opportunities for risky play *what is the importance of documentation*?
Within a program, the documentation of risky play policies and procedures are key to providing consistent and safe support to the children. It allows program administrators, teachers, volunteers, and parents to all be on the same page about what is allowed or expected from children and adult behavior. They can be developed by the community, or by a leader within the community, and then used for training purposes. It will also be important to review and improve the policies and procedures as conditions or seasons change, or if the program is taking place in an area with different environmental hazards. Some programs here in WA will also take into consideration the various children's developmental levels, abilities, and daily check-ins of behavior to ensure their risky play management is as safe and responsive as possible. Such individualized and reflective attention to risk management is indeed a best practice in benefit-risk assessment.

Documentation is also essential for oversight, and so that governments can ensure that a program is supporting risky play safely. When licensing an early learning program, a government provides an assurance to their citizens that a business is safe for the children. Most families are not able to observe the program, or would be unable to find alternative childcare even if they wanted, and so the government assumes that responsibility to ensure the program is safe and supportive of children's development. Licensing regulations are always made with the intended purpose of protecting children, families, providers, and keeping everyone accountable in a fair and consistent way. So when a program is offering risky play activities, documenting the planned practices is essential for a licensing agency to ensure the program takes child safety seriously and can support risky play appropriately.

How/why can documenting injuries be a part of your risky play documentation?
We also expect programs to keep a record of any injuries or incidents, such as a missing child, and report serious occurrences to the licensing office. This goes for any licensed childcare, and is part of the responsibility of an oversight agency/ government to protect children. What most often happens is that a licensor or investigator (depending on the nature or seriousness of the injury) would come to the program to learn more and then help in the appropriate way. For a risky play injury (like a concussion or broken bone), we would come to the program to review their policies and procedures, take a look at where the injury occurred, and generally find out what happened that day. We would then provide technical assistance on how to improve, or if it really was a case of neglect (like leaving a child unsupervised) take an enforcement action to ensure child safety. Keep in mind that many licensors once worked in the field of early childhood education and are also visiting many programs throughout your region. Licensors come with a wealth of knowledge and have some great practices to share, albeit with a different lens and responsibility.

How/why should a program communicate its risky play policies (from director to staff to parents) in trainings/ handbooks, etc?
In addition to carrying out benefit-risk assessments and creating related risky play policies and procedures, here in Washington we also expect a program's director to keep a record that staff have been trained on these policies and procedures, and that parents are aware of and agree to the programs' rules and philosophies. The best time to share and ensure a shared understanding of these things is right at the beginning of the connection, whether that be prior to hiring or prior to enrollment. People need to know what they're getting into, in the same way you share a program's philosophy and program schedule, the approach to risky play is an important part of that process. In addition, this should be reviewed periodically, and especially seasonally for outdoor nature-based programs, to make sure people still agree, or if there any changes that need to be made. As mentioned above, policies and procedures should especially be reviewed if there are any incidents or serious injuries that occur.

Other advice/ideas from the regulation-licensing point of view to help programs feel more comfortable with trying risky play?
It is important to also understand that every individual adult's comfort with risky play will be different. By focusing on the benefits as well as the risks, you can think about solutions that still provide children with the benefits, while still being sensitive to different adults' views. Starting with the intention of trying it, and having regular (and honest) check-ins and reviews, is a great way to build trust and also cultivate best practices for both teachers and licensors. Recognize, however, that licensors are responsible for ensuring laws and regulations are consistently implemented, and so they may not have the flexibility you want. If you need to change the regulations in order to be able to support risky play that you find necessary for your philosophy of children's education, then be prepared to support your views and allow the licensing agency/government to collect data and ensure that you are, in fact, correct in your thinking and practices.

PART 4

Program Tour

Everybody Ready?

Now it's time to take you on a tour of some of my favorite play spots on the planet. Let's see this stuff in action. I've been hinting at "all outdoor nature schools" and "loose parts playgrounds" but you really have to see for yourself. I love visiting wild play spaces and being surprised by what the adults and children are up to. It's inspiring to see paradigms pushed and how well it can all work. At first things might seem crazy or over the top, but the more we can look with fresh eyes and open hearts (and deep breaths) the easier it is to see that these places are actually completely, absolutely "normal." Kids being kids. Nature being nature. And adults being adults who get it, support it, and say yes to play.

So join me now on a tour of the right-side up world…

Nature Kindergarten
SCOTLAND

Being involved in nature play and play spaces I am always excited to learn about great things happening in different parts of the world. For years I heard mythical stories about all-outdoor schools in faraway lands where children spend entire days outside in the woods in all kinds of weather in all seasons of the year. The stories were always about people in Norway or some such place doing these amazing things with children bundled up in puffy snow suits spending the days among ice and snow exploring the frozen tundra and laughing at the cold with that famous motto, "no bad weather, just bad clothing." *All outdoor schools? In all weather? In the forest? Children whittling? Playing with fire??* It all sounded outrageous and wonderful at first. But true? Turns out: yes. As years went by I heard more and more reports of these hearty places and dreamed of seeing them for myself. (A German neighbor of mine shared the story that her nephew back in the old country received a pocket knife from his school for his 5th birthday. Sounds crazy until you realize that he too attended a "forest school" and had been safely using knives to carve wood and prepare meals since he was three. Oh yeah, children with care and guidance are capable of amazing things.)

Low and behold during a World Forum Nature Action Collaborative for Children symposium at Arbor Day Farm in Nebraska I heard a wild woman from Scotland talk about her own nature kindergartens with fires, trees, mud, kids, and all outdoor days with good clothing and good humor. Her stories sounded amazing and the pictures she showed were eye-opening. The wild woman was Claire Warden of Mindstretchers, Ltd., based in Crieff, Scotland. She was leading a new wave of nature play experiences for preschool children with best practices and protocols weaving nature education with open-ended play, child-led projects, and infinite possibilities through daily excursions in nature. She travels the world speaking and inspiring educators to expand their thinking and allowances for children's play and learning in nature.

A few years after meeting and recognizing we were kindred spirits, I had the great opportunity to visit her sites and I jumped at the chance to spend time with Claire and see her nature kindergarten concepts up close. What a treat! This next section shows what I experienced and saw. Back then for many of us this was new territory, but I will tell you that at the time of writing this book there are currently over 250 forest school programs in North America alone.[13] The ideas of Claire and the Northern Europeans are being celebrated and embraced around the world and incorporated into children's lives in ways big and small. Slip on your muck boots, pull on your rain pants, and let's visit Claire's kindergartens, tag along with her exploring children, and see what the hubbub is all about…

Like a pilgrim in the promised land I found myself walking toward the gate of the famous Auchlone Nature Kindergarten. Classroom headquarters is a former gatehouse made of ancient stone on the edge of a vast estate updated with modern amenities. The formal fenced-in playscape is filled with everything I love: bumpy rugged hills, rocks, sand, living willow huts, trees, grass, and dirt. I also noted a loose parts play corner and raised fire pit—and that the perimeter fence didn't stop at the edge of the actual forest. Instead, it went inside the forest to scoop out a part of the woods and offer it to children any time they wanted to visit. So great!

Headquarters outside is their beautiful, semi-enclosed, timber-framed "kitchen" structure with running water, an oven, tables, chairs and lounging areas, and a wood stove to keep the place cozy on chillier days. It's the perfect place for snack time, naps, baking bread, doing art projects, eating lunch, group meetings, washing hands, reading a book or just hanging out. The daytime flow happened naturally in and out of the kitchen and playscape according to children's wishes and inclinations.

Program Tour 189

As is the tradition when one child feels ready and the adults and rest of the kids agree, "woods time" is called and they all line up for an excursion into the vast forest land outside the fence. I noticed the line forming, joined with the crew, and followed them into the woods.

The adults started out cautiously and carefully with multiple stops to get head counts and make sure everybody was together as we began our journey into the trees. Part of the daily expedition is a "woods wagon" they pull along filled with everything they might need for the day: water, snacks, first aid kit, plates, utensils and assorted tools and surprises.

Once we were all together and ready we plunged our way into the trees and followed a well-worn trail into the heart of this old forest. At some point I realized that we were "there." A variety of features showed themselves to me with signs of kid-erosion and love. A fallen tree trimmed up for safety and ropes and a tire hanging from a tree let me know that teachers had made subtle interventions to create a playful gathering area and a welcoming sense of place.

The headquarters of this area was a beautiful hand-crafted gazebo-style structure with open air entrances and a circular opening in the center of the roof. What could this opening be for I wondered? To let the smoke from the central fire pit out of course! Inside were benches and another raised fire pit. Today's snack was to be pancakes cooked over the open fire. With the guidance of a teacher children were entrusted to use a flint set to get the fire started by spark and tissue paper. (Once the fire was started this group had the rule of kids staying on the outside of the log square arranged on the ground around the fire pit.)

Program Tour 193

Trails lead to other fun locations. A small stream flowing gently through the woods is a favorite place to visit. Children helped decide rules for stream safety and exploration. Watching water and poking rocks with sticks offers endless fascination.

There was a calm in the air and a presence of being a part of something sacred, living, and larger than ourselves. The children felt a part of the forest and the forest was a part of them too. What was happening here was groundbreaking and new but at the same time simple, ancient, and obvious. Human children have been in the woods and nature for as long as there have been humans. Our bodies and minds were made to be in the wilds. We are a part of the planet earth. We, like trees, are earthlings, kin, related, and part of the family of life. Seeing the children carefree in this setting felt as natural as anything I'd ever been a part of. In fact, it felt more natural and calm and right to me than any man-made classroom or playground that children are typically forced to inhabit. What could children learn in a setting like this? Could the peace of nature soothe the needs of all children? Could it help solve attention and hyperactive tendencies? Could time spent in nature be the gift that boosts spirits and souls for children and adults alike? These children were certainly thriving in nature. The adults seemed happy too.

I know we can't all have ancient Scottish woodlands to visit with our children, but perhaps seeing how well children do in these settings can inspire us to think about where we can bring our children to experience the healing and beauty of the natural world. Do you have parkland nearby your site? Are there neighbors with land that might let you visit? Are you on a college campus or is there a vacant lot you could easily explore? Some places need your beforehand scouting and removal of hazards and excess debris. Some places just need to be asked for permission. Planting a forest within your fenced playground can recreate the wonders of wild lands. Planted trees and shrubs invite birds and bugs and from there your start to build a new ecosystem. This ecosystem is the system we are all a part of. It is where we come from and the place where children thrive.

CLAIRE WARDEN
Auchlone Nature Kindergarten
Crieff, Scotland

Share a little bit about the philosophy of Auchlone.
Auchlone Nature Kindergarten is the manifestation of our values of love, hope and justice that we as a team believe in. We support place-based learning as it gives us meaning and a history making potential that is valued by children and families. The situation has a home styled inside area in an 17th Century stone house, a landscape designed by children with hills, hiding spaces and a mud fest area. This links seamlessly to the area beyond the fence where the natural landscape of fields and forests is on nature's terms, not cleaned up or tidied away.

What does a day in the program look like?
At Auchlone, children are outside 70-100% of the time all year round, five days a week if they want to be. Given the damp climate here in Scotland we sometimes settle in an open fronted KinderKitchen that allows daily cooking, warmth from a log stove and light from a child-created stick candelabra. It is in this space, where we stay in our outdoor clothes, that we develop a real sense of community, resting after a strenuous walk or sharing our tales of risk and adventure.

There are many routines that are often the backbone of our daily and seasonal rhythms. Collecting wood for the fire, harvesting food, making our felt slippers, packing back packs for our journeys, designing and making forts and shelters and celebrating the joy and love of it all through story, song and making artifacts. There are those that suggest that there is an unrealistic romantic notion of

childhood and nature presented in a nature kindergarten. In my research, I assert that although childhoods are indeed situated and complex, there is a purity in the moment where a child studies a worm or is fascinated by water droplets on a leaf that exists below these larger lived worlds[11].

How do you navigate risk, as part of your program?
Our nature kindergarten has received the highest ratings by the inspectorate for care and education. This is as a result of the staff training in Nature Pedagogy that supports them to understand and connect to how to learn with nature rather than just be in it, or learn about it. The pedagogy and landscape have become intertwined in a way that they work seamlessly together. Children and families feel it when they come to be with us, it's a relational pedagogy that places value on all living and non-living aspects of early education. The ratios we work with are 1:8 for 3-5 years and this doesn't alter across spaces unless we are near water, as we don't perceive there to be more hazards outside, in fact the reverse is true.

We have built on Tim Gill's work, so that the risk management process records children's voices and their ideas as the stake holders, dynamic risk assessments that change daily and residual risk assessments that are written up for the site itself and the experience offered[12]. Rather than risk assessments preventing adventure we suggest that they enable us to think collectively as a team and therefore support us to give children the freedom they seek. The physicality and complexity of the nature kindergarten allow the body, brain and soul to grow. The range of simple materials provide complex learning through a range of provocations that authentically emerge from the context.

Wild Woods

NEW ZEALAND

I've heard my whole life that New Zealand is the most beautiful place in the world. I always took it with a grain of salt thinking, "yeah, yeah, come on, it's beautiful everywhere"…until I had the chance to visit myself. It is beautiful. Incredible landscapes, beaches, farmland, mountains, thermal creeks, millions of sheep, and good-natured people with deep connections to the land. I fell in love with the place (and had to seriously talk myself back into taking that return flight home). It felt like a place where you could really be true to yourself. Now, I'm sure there are ups and downs like everywhere and I know my trip was colored by the incredible people and places I was able to visit and connect with. I spent lots of time with educators and was inspired over and over by their passions for children, respect and inclusion of the indigenous Maori people and culture in society and education systems, and their dedication to creating ecological spaces for children's play and learning.

My trip was also colored because the whole thing began at my favorite conference in the world, the Natural Phenomena conference held in Whangarei way up north— hosted by Open Spaces Preschool and their supercharged director Cherry Daly. The only conference (so far) that I've keynoted barefoot in the grass, the whole weekend is held outdoors around fires, under tents, beside ancient trees, participants camping and playing music, building fairy huts and nature sculptures and bonding over something we all deeply believe in: connecting children to nature and saying yes to play. I was in heaven. But I was also charged up because I had spent days previous with Cherry and her dedicated teachers on their wonderful natural playground and… tagging along with classes in her nature kindergarten-inspired "Wild Woods."

Cherry runs her Open Spaces Preschool on her family's farm property. The farm once trained race horses and her uncle was a prize-winning dog sheep herder. As you can see by her play yard Cherry's child development philosophy was connected to the outdoors and nature. But it was after she attended a Nature Action Collaborative conference in Nebraska and heard Claire Warden speak so passionately about the beauty of nature kindergartens that Cherry decided she wanted to have

a nature kindergarten or forest school of her own. But where could she do it? As she dreamed the possibilities she realized she had a beautiful opportunity right on her family's farm! And lo and behold, with her family's blessing she began taking children to an incredible spot on the land for outdoor exploration in a couple acres of their ancient forest. When I visited, teachers were bringing small groups from their classes to the woods every day. I had the privilege of joining one group on a summer's day as they explored the "Wild Woods."

The walk along the dirt farm road to the woods was a fun adventure in itself with puddles and bugs and horses to pet along the way. But then something magical happened when we walked through the gateway into the woods. The energy shifted, the children got quiet, and they began to explore and play with concentrated child-like wonder and awe. I wish I had a thousand-year-old tree to play around and hug. These children do. They climb and hide and look for treasures. Fallen trees provide balance and self-trust opportunities. Spider eggs and bugs under stumps are sources of delight, questions, excitement and focus. Lunch outside. Pretend play. Walking on roots. Petting pigs. It's a beautiful scene to behold.

Program Tour 201

GEOFF FUGLE, Lead Educator
Open Spaces Preschool
Whangarei, New Zealand

How do the children use the woods space?
The wild woods offer many different things to the children: it is physically challenging, free from control and structure, it is a place of wonder and discovery, a source and an inspiration for many games, a place for hypothesizing, solitude, the edge of comfort. Getting 'lost' is both scary and exciting.

What are your thoughts on play + risk + nature?
We factor for about 50% of our time in the woods to be 'free play'—the rest of the time there is a subtle teacher agenda at work. We may just go wandering, follow our trails (even work on repairing them), or head to a favorite destination like the creek or the climbing tree. All the time we teachers are modeling risk assessment—a core part of our woods program. The environment is full of risks and falling/tripping is top of the list. We constantly vocalize our thoughts around risk assessment and keeping ourselves safe: *"The stream looks deep here, I might look for another place to cross." "Wow that rock feels slippery, I'm going to use my hands for this bit,"* etc.

Nature is the perfect playground because nothing is standardized and thus careful thinking is required to move about in it. In the woods we must watch every step, assess where to put our hands next, check for stability, strength, etc. It's a sensory-rich environment that demands attention.

What lessons have you learned?
Keep it simple, consistent, fun. Don't alter the environment to be a playground. Don't be afraid of risks. Protect yourselves from unnecessary risk: create policy guidelines, perform hazard checks, do benefit/risk analysis, create first aid procedures, etc. Don't get hung up on 'outcomes.' Create a resource-rich base from which to explore. Here we have art supplies, books, tools, toilet, eating area, etc.

How has the use of the space evolved over time?
It has moved from a largely unstructured and fragmented approach to its current fuller potential. Professional development has shown us how a balance of child-led play and collaborative nature-based teaching offers the most potential. The work of Ann Pelo and *The Coyote Guide* offer us much in how we as teachers can get the most out of nature: rituals, play, science, imaginations, culture, family links, dispositional learning, etc.

What advice do you have for others wanting to say yes more to children's nature play and risk?
Just do it. Read a lot, go to your nature space alone and explore it—find the good and the bad, start off small and develop from there...

Adventure School
ITHACA, NEW YORK

The movement to connect children to nature is growing and adults everywhere are working to get children in touch with all things good in the natural world. Some people are creating natural playscapes within their backyards and playgrounds. Other folks take their children straight to the wild lands themselves. Forest schools and nature kindergartens are established institutions of nature play and learning but you can do the same thing in your own community just by deciding to do it. This next chapter shows what some of my neighbors and friends and I set up for our young children a few years ago: we called it "Adventure School."

Adventure School started out like lots of things do, with dreamy conversations among adults. What if our kids could get together on a regular basis and play in nature? What if preschool was an all-outside experience? What if adults just helped around the edges but let the children lead their own adventures? What if we had a preschool that took place in creeks or by the fire? What if there was such a thing in our town? Someone should start a school or playgroup like that. Ok, let's do it!

And so we did: Adventure School was born. About eight families were involved coming from different situations of homeschooling, un-schooling, preschooling, stay at home parents, work at home parents, etc. We set up a rotation of locations at each of our houses and homesteads (country folks were we). Some families lived on farms. Others lived in the woods. Some families had creeks. Others had wide open meadows. There were lots of amazing places to explore so we set up a plan to have a different site host each time and proceeded to have an informal-formal play group that met consistently 1-2 days a week experiencing a variety of seasons, weather, and natural scenes.

We wanted our children connecting with other kids and getting to do all the great play stuff we've been talking about in this book: mixed-ages, barefoot kids, tree climbing, fire building, chickens, loose parts, risk, water, rough and tumble and more. Supervision was loose but effective. The host parents would be on-site with a couple of adult helpers having fun and keeping a general eye on things. Children explored trails, tromped through creeks, played in leaves, built forts, zoomed down hills on wheeled vehicles, balanced on logs, made art, cooked over fires, had snowball fights, made snow sculptures, and lots more. The set up was simple, the system low-key.

Program Tour 209

Could you do something similar with families in your community? Could classes go out on more regular "nature play field trips" to nearby natural areas? Are there places like parks or vacant lots you could look into getting permission to visit? Anything within walking distance? Could families drop off and pick up in remote locations? Could parents be a part of the fun with a co-op style rotation of play chaperones? The natural world is definitely awaiting you and your children—ready, willing and able to host!

Swedish Open-Air School

MALMO, SWEDEN

What if a school took this belief in nature, play, risk and connections to the outdoors for children to heart? It might look like the independent "open-air" Skabersjoskolan outside Malmo, Sweden, whose pedagogical goals consist of outdoor education, outdoor life, experience-based learning and conscious leadership. This is a school that values and prioritizes time spent outdoors as much as it utilizes its time spent indoors. I spent time visiting the school as part of a "Nordic Adventure Play" symposium and got to see firsthand the practical and engaging schoolyard where children preschool through fifth grade spend their days. They eat outside, have lessons outside, meet as a school outside, and of course have recess and play time outside. The school grounds are a combination of open, multi-use grassy lawns, simple fitness equipment, woodsy play areas, formal vegetable gardens with raised planters, outdoor classrooms, fire pits, play houses, sand pits, storage sheds, and a planted forest lining the back border filled with loose play materials and evidence of deep, child-led play. What if all schools supported outdoor play and learning like Skabersjoskolan?

Hudson Valley Sudbury School

WOODSTOCK, NEW YORK

I knew something was different about this school the first time they contacted me. The woman on the phone—Vanessa—was inquiring about my playscape design services; she was calling on behalf of the kids at her school. It was the kids who had decided they wanted to work with me to help them with their projects. Vanessa told me that this was a unique school where the students directed their own education and that this was a kid-initiated project. They wanted an update to their play yard, wanted to build it themselves, and wanted to hire a professional to work with them. After doing their own research I was the professional they chose and could I help them come up with a plan and assist them in construction? My immediate answer: Wow! And yes!

So we plotted and planned like any project and geared ourselves toward a big volunteer construction day. They had a small budget and big plans and looked to use as much donated and scrounged local materials as they could get. We broke down the design into small projects that teams could tackle and I would work with the youth builders as they constructed their own forts and features in the woods adjacent to the school building. This was new for me and I was excited. During a lot of my projects children might be helpers, but with construction being slightly dangerous (and I'm often working in early childhood settings) children are often kept near the sidelines.

Not with this school. The students were front and center and I was to be their helper. My job was to keep an eye on things, help with tools, build strong structural elements that they could build off of, etc. This was my first time being a part of something that felt like those European adventure playgrounds I like to visit—where children build their own structures with saws and hammers and adult playworkers helping out around the edges. Here was my first opportunity to really build with kids. As I did, my ideas about education, children's rights, and self-direction were flipped on their head. Not only did this school present a different model of what education could look like, it showed me an entirely different way of being with children in the world.

Program Tour 217

The children at this school were self-directed learners. That is, they followed their own desires and instincts as to what they wanted to learn about and pursue. There are no grades at this school, no grade levels, no classes, no actual "teachers." The entire school is run democratically with children's voices honored and listened to. This was no "un-school." The building's facilities were impressive. They sported a fine library, computer lab, music rooms, a cozy living room, lounge area, art room, offices, and a large-scale kitchen. Adults were part of the action but only as facilitators and helpers to the children as they made their way through their days. Mixed-age was an understatement here: kindergarteners run alongside not only school-agers but middle school and high school age students. And children choose what they want to do all day every day. If you want to be outdoors playing four-square all day you were free to do it. All week even if you were feeling so moved. You could be on the computer, baking bread, reading books, drawing, sewing, playing video games, talking with your friends, or participating in an all-school disciplinary meeting to debate rules and consequences in a respectful democratic manner.

Or, on this day, you could choose to be out on in the woods with Rusty Keeler building stuff. Many kids did join me and together we spent the day building, creating, and having a lot of fun. For these students the project was their idea and their passion. But the playground construction wasn't everybody's passion and nobody was forced to participate. Students here did what they wanted, when they wanted. This alone was a new concept for me. While students led the project, other children would wander in and help now and then. Other kids would swing by to watch the progress. And still others could not have cared less what was going on outside that day and paid no attention at all. On a break I walked through the school with my lemonade and sure enough, there were kids reading books on the couch, talking in groups, listening to music, playing games with (gasp) no interest in building play stuff with me!

After my ego was done feeling bruised my mind was blown: nobody was forcing kids to do anything they didn't want to do. In a traditional school setting I could imagine an adult marching the whole class out to where I was set up in the woods, where the children would be forced to listen to me talk about the project, then forced to participate and held to some standard of action and behavior according to adults' ideas, wishes, and timeframes (or concept of what children should be doing). At this school, children themselves had the power to determine what they should be doing, when, and for how long. What? Whoa.

It goes against, well, everything that traditional school models stand for. It goes against the adult-down model of most interactions adults have with children. These kids weren't talked down to and pushed into situations they'd rather not be in. They chose for themselves. Now I get it: not everyone wants to build a playground…and why should they? Everybody had the opportunity to join the construction that day but not everybody did because not everybody was interested. And if you are not interested in being somewhere why should you be forced? Is it good for you? Is it good for the project? **What are children's rights and how do we support them?** And conversely, how do we squash children's rights when we decide and plan their opportunities, ideas, activities, interests and their uses of time.

It's enough to make even the most well-meaning pro-child adult take a long look at themselves in the mirror and question all our interactions with children. Being at this school certainly threw me for a loop. **Do we "adulterate" children's lives?** Do we mostly dictate what they do, when, with whom, and how? Without a doubt.

Look at it from a child's rights point of view. If we treated adults the way we treat children, well, it could seem criminal. Power-hungry. Controlling. It's almost like we're holding them hostage without freedom to decide what's best for themselves. Whew.

And yet here are examples of institutions that are reversing this trend. Every time you allow a child to balance on a log or take some moderate risk you are supporting children's freedom. We all love early childhood settings that follow the child, are project-driven, are inspired by artistic Reggio Emilia models. They feel right when we see them in action because the child is a more front and center part of the curriculum and learning. The adults work hard to find and follow the children's interests and ideas and support them to see where they go. You gotta love it. But then you have to soak it up because early childhood doesn't last forever and children must move on to higher stages of education. Parents of Reggio-inspired schools and nature preschools often say the same thing: "what happens next for my child? Are there no models of similar styles for older children?" I admit that seeing the Hudson Valley Sudbury School in action was jarring and confusing at first—it's not what you expect from an adult-driven typical school— but the more time I spent with the self-confident, able students, and the more interactions I saw with the supportive adults, the more it gave me a picture of what a school could be like if it continued that child-led, Reggio-ish practice of honoring and supporting the child and their rights. It's strange to witness at first, but then it soon feels completely natural, normal, and freeing.

Can we work to honor children's rights and support their ideas and decision-making even within the most traditional systems? Yes. Like all this stuff, we can dream big and start small. It can start with letting go on the playground. It can start with extending schedules. It can start with loose parts and open-ended materials. It can start with really listening to what children want and need and asking, "How can I help? How can I support you?" Maybe they'll give you a "Best Supporting Adult" award if you keep it up!

Our playscape build days were a blast. All kids present were enthusiastic and ready for action with a whole range of skill levels, ages, and talents in the mix. We hauled materials, picked locations, and commenced to build. We did it again the next year and the following year too. From what I hear they do a spring build every year now based on the original plans, what everyone decides they want to construct next, and what materials can be gleaned from the community.

And I had another life-changing epiphany: tires=good. I must admit as a natural playscape designer, I preferred all things natural. "No tires, no plastic, no junk—only natural materials for children." Once again this group of independent kids changed my mind! Back then I was thinking only of tires being used to build the playground, not as loose parts for kid construction. One group of children chose as a job to scrub the donated tires that we had on hand. I paid little attention and went about my business in the woods. After a while I came out and those tire kids had built the most amazing tire sculpture-castle. A little while later they were having games rolling tires around the yard. A while later they had built towers, spaceships, who knows what. Suddenly I was sold: tires are awesome, endless, loose parts play materials. I can admit when I'm wrong. Now you can often find me driving around my home town with a trunk full of odd-sized tires delivering them to the local elementary schools for loose parts recess play. I've seen the light!

These kid-led build days really showed me what kids can do with a little guidance, a lot of trust, friendly support, and fun collaborations. With kids respected and allowed to do as they wish, and with adults supporting their visions playworker-style, the Hudson Valley Sudbury School was like an adventure playground that turned itself into a school… then turned its yard into an adventure playground!

PETER GRAY,
Research Professor of Psychology, Boston College
Chestnut Hill, Massachusetts, United States

Peter Gray is an expert in the Self-Directed Education model that the Hudson Valley Sudbury School practices and author of <u>Free to Learn: Why Unleashing the Instinct to Play Will Make Our Children Happier, More Self-Reliant, and Better Students for Life</u> (Basic Books, 2013), and founder and board president of Alliance for Self-Directed Education. I asked Peter to share some thoughts on this intriguing style of education.

What is Self-Directed Education?
I like to define "education" as the sum total of what a person learns that helps that person live a satisfying and meaningful life. With that definition, "self-directed education" (with lower-case letters) is education that comes in the course of life, by pursuing one's own interests and meeting the challenges of life itself. Then, "Self-Directed Education" (capital letters) refers to the deliberate choice to take charge of one's own education, to learn through following one's own interests, without an imposed curriculum. People attending a school or learning center designed to enable them to pursue their own interests (without an imposed curriculum or evaluation) or engaged in homeschooling (unschooling) with no imposed curriculum or testing are engaged in Self-Directed Education.

Why is it good for children?
Children are naturally designed for self-directed education. Their curiosity, playfulness, sociability, willfulness, and natural desire to do well in life have been shaped by natural selection to ensure that they will, when free and when provided with appropriate life opportunities, learn what they need to know to live satisfying and meaningful lives in the culture in which they are growing. Children in Self-Directed Education retain their love of learning, sense of control over their own lives, and sense of personal responsibility, which are often driven out of children who are forced to study what does not interest them. In schools children all too often learn that the purpose of life is to go through one meaningless hoop after another rather than to find and pursue activities that are truly meaningful to them.

What does it look like?
It looks like life.

How do adults support children's Self-Directed Education?
Children navigate but adults provide the pond within which they navigate. It's a bit like an adventure playground, where the children play as they wish but the playworkers provide the materials and remove the more dangerous hazards.

My research suggests that the ideal environmental conditions for Self-Directed Education include the following:

1. The social expectation (and reality) that education is children's responsibility.

2. Unlimited freedom to play, explore, and pursue one's own interests.

3. Opportunity to play with the tools of the culture.

4. Access to a variety of caring adults, who are helpers, not judges.

5. Free age mixing among children and adolescents. Younger children learn by watching, overhearing, and interacting with older ones, and older children acquire nurturing and leadership abilities by interacting with younger ones.

6. Immersion in a stable, moral, caring, democratic community, as this helps children feel safe, feel that their opinions count, and understand that they are responsible not just for themselves but also for the larger community of which they are a part.

How many schools can say these conditions are present?

How can people new to the concept incorporate ideas/ philosophy into their daily practice at, say, traditional public schools and childcare centers?
The best thing that people at traditional schools can do to foster self-directed education is to reduce, rather than continuously increase, the amount of time that children have to spend at school and homework. Children in traditional schools can educate themselves when they are not at school, but to do so they need time and freedom outside of school.

What about children learning Math? Reading? Don't they need adults making sure they learn these things? (etc. etc.)
The short answer is that children growing up in a literate and numerate environment pick up reading and calculation ability in the same basic ways that they pick up everything else. Those who decide to pursue interests that require more complex math—of the sort that few people use in everyday life—deliberately and efficiently learn the math they need. Today this is easier than ever, as there are many online courses and websites to help.

Adventure Playgrounds

My favorite built environments for children's self-directed play? Adventure Playgrounds. You may have seen images of these seemingly crazy places: wild, rickety, kid-built scrap wood structures towering above any possibility of playground safety surfacing, with kids cooking over fires, digging in the dirt, keeping animals, and tending gardens.

The history of adventure playgrounds is quite fascinating. What started as a pet project by a Danish designer soon picked up steam and became a popular model for children's playspaces across Europe in the years following World War II (and beyond).

For many of us these "Junk Playgrounds" sound a lot like our own adventurous childhoods. I certainly remember seeing stuff like this in the culture as a kid of the 1970's. Home grown, pallet-built, earthy, rootsy, play stuff. As a kid growing up in the United States it felt like there was a child and earth-first spirit in the air with adults and educators working to support innovative new models of play and learning. It was a good time to be bell-bottomed and ten with time and freedom to play and explore. While primarily a European movement there were still a fair number of adventure playgrounds in North America and life was good.

Then somewhere along the line as we've been exploring in this book, society changed, cleaned up its act and put higher focus on perceived safety and tightened guidelines for play. At the same time many of our domestic adventure playgrounds fell by the wayside and colorful, commercialized, industrial fixed playground equipment became the norm for children's spaces. This continued for decades and as time went on a false narrative and belief system around adventure playgrounds took hold with the common notion that these dangerous-seeming places fizzled because of our current over-protected, highly litigious society. Yet at the same time many people kept the adventure playground spirit alive. Although there were always ups and downs in the European world of adventure playgrounds, they survived and thrived, providing generations of children opportunities for freedom and play. At the same time, the profession of playwork was developed and refined. Dedicated on-site staff learned to recognize, celebrate and support children's play in all its fundamental forms. Fast forward to our current era and we finds ourselves in an adventure playground renaissance. Yes! Adventure Play projects are popping up all over and a whole new movement is upon us to support risky play spaces that say yes to children's self-directed play and no to overprotectedness. New research and inquiry[14] has shown us that the earlier North American adventure playground movement didn't stop because of lawsuits and insurance issues but because of more mundane reasons like land leases expired, founding members moved on, organizational funds were reallocated, etc. Bolstered by this knowledge, inspired by images and tours of the current European adventure playgrounds, and cheered on by friends in the playworker world, pockets of people from all corners of life began taking steps to start a new wave of adventure playgrounds. These spaces support children in their own communities and are models for the world that children can be trusted and supported to thrive (and survive) life in adventure playgrounds. In fact, children may need these environments now more than ever!

This chapter is a brief look at the history of adventure playgrounds and a tour of current inspirational models of European, Australian, and North American adventure playgrounds.

History

Landscape Architect Carl Theodor Sørensen is credited with creating the first planned adventure playground in Emdrup outside of Copenhagen, Denmark in 1943. After noticing that children preferred playing in construction sites and empty lots over his carefully-designed playgrounds he began thinking about spaces where children could be free to build and create what they wanted with a wide range of loose materials, rather than a fixed playground where the play was prescribed by the designer or manufacturer. Sørensen envisioned empty lots filled with loose parts galore, giving children ultimate freedom to construct according to their wishes. He called these first playgrounds "junk playgrounds" because of the use of discarded scrap materials. He was also aiming to give city children the same open-ended play opportunities that he felt country children had and loose messy play possibilities were at the heart of it all. As a play designer I love Sørensen's later reflections on those playgrounds, **"Of all the things I have helped to realize, the Junk Playground is the ugliest; yet for me it is the best and most beautiful of my works."** We know exactly what he means. Children at play with endless possibilities before them are a beautiful thing to behold.

At this same time adults throughout Europe were witnessing a similar style of play in the loose rubble of bomb sites. With bricks, boards, rocks and other found materials children tapped the healing properties of play as they re-emerged into their lives after the frightening experiences of the war. Marjory Allen, (Lady Allen of Hurtwood) an English landscape architect and advocate for children's rights and welfare, is credited for bringing the junk playground concept to England. During a trip to Copenhagen she was deeply moved by the playground at Emdrup and returned home eager to create similar environments for children in the United Kingdom. In an article about Emdrup titled "Why Not Use Our Bomb Sites Like This?" Lady Allen later wrote, "*I was completely swept off my feet by my first visit to Emdrup playground. In a flash of understanding I realized that I was looking at something quite new and full of possibilities. There was a wealth of waste material on it and no man-made fixtures. The children could dig, build houses, experiment with sand, water or fire and play games of adventure and make believe.*" With hard work the concept took hold and adults began cleaning up the bomb sites for general safety and introducing tools, loose materials, and water as well. Adult playworkers were carefully selected for their ability to support children's rights and free play. The newly coined term "adventure playground" gained popularity (better for PR than junk playground apparently) and these sites quickly spread to other similar cities after World War II.

We have the great opportunity to glimpse this amazing early world of adventure playgrounds through the photographic lens of United Kingdom playworker and child's rights advocate Donne Buck. Originally from New Zealand, Donne moved to the United Kingdom in the 1950's and became one of the first professional playworkers starting at an adventure playground at a converted bomb site in Hackney, England. He went on to design, set up and operate numerous adventure playgrounds across England throughout his career and captured scenes of adventure play with his camera for more than six decades. His photographs have become a significant national legacy and the photos you see here are part of his much-loved archive currently housed at the Victoria and Albert Museum in London. I've had the pleasure of becoming friends with Donne through my excitement and interest in adventure playgrounds and he has generously us given permission to reprint his pictures in this book and agreed to share some personal thoughts on adventure play.

PHOTO BY DONNE BUCK

DONNE BUCK
New Ark Adventure Playground & City Farm
Peterborough, United Kingdom

Why is there a need for adventure playgrounds and what do children gain from them?
Science shows us that, simply expressed, play is the child's inbuilt way of learning about the world, themselves and other people. Adults can support or restrict it, but, if children are to develop to their full potential, they need the fullest possible freedom to explore their social and physical environments from their early years. Modern living tends to severely restrict play opportunities with dire consequences for child development. The experience of offering adventure playgrounds to children in a very wide range of settings all over the world has shown that they immediately respond to the freedom to play in a secure environment and the benefits of this high quality play are reflected in the rest of their lives.

What were adventure playgrounds like in the early days and how has playwork evolved?
What Emdrup and the early London adventure playgrounds had in common was that they were enclosed outdoor sites with access to shelter and utilities nearby or on-site, were staffed by at least one adult with an understanding of children's play and offered a wide range of loose materials, tools and changes of level. They were open for the longterm, children were free to come and go and all age groups had access. Most of the London playgrounds were on demolition sites resulting from World War II, which meant that they often contained bricks and other debris which could be adapted for play use. Each playground was an independent charity managed by volunteers, funded for running costs, including staffing, from a variety of sources including grants from other charities and public authorities, local fundraising and donations in kind. Most on-site support came from volunteers, including parents, students and retired people.

How did you get into the playwork profession? Well, there was no such term or work when I started. I came into it by accident. My intention in coming to London, England from New Zealand in 1956 was to find welfare work with needy families, perhaps as a social worker. However I soon found that this was closed to me due to my lack of qualifications and experience. So I began an extramural university course in sociology and took work in a hospital and booksellers and hoped that something would turn up. Within a few months it did. Through other friends I met the headteacher of a primary school in the East End of London who had been asked to help with the setting of a play project opposite her school.

Why do children need to experience free play and risk?
No amount of telling children how to behave and to avoid accidents can replace direct experience of the physical world and of direct dealings with people and other living things. Playgrounds that offer a wide range of experience, including experience of risk, on secure sites under the guidance of playworkers, such as adventure playgrounds are, I believe, the best.

How can other professionals can be inspired by playwork?
Well, I suppose that there are two ways, first by including playwork literature in their training and second by setting up projects like pop-up supervised play facilities and visiting high quality existing projects. There is a great deal of adventure playground literature around in English, starting perhaps with Lady Allen of Hurtwoods' booklets Planning for Play and Adventure Playgrounds and her biography *Memoirs of an Uneducated Lady* which are in my archive.

How can people introduce more child-directed play to the people they work with? This is a tricky one as there is a tendency for practitioners in one area to see others as rivals, threatening the basis and resources of their own work. When working as a teacher I found other teachers very reluctant to accept my using playwork methods as part of my classroom technique. This did not stop me

Program Tour   229

PHOTOS BY DONNE BUCK, CURATED BY MORGAN LEICHTER-SAXBY

trying, but I often found myself at odds with colleagues, especially the more senior ones and headteachers, though my own teacher training included a strong emphasis on play methods. Within public authorities that provide more formal leisure and sporting services, playworkers tend to be despised and deprived of resources, even when their work is clearly appreciated by the children and supported by parents and the community at large. Since other professionals tend be highly resistant to adopting playwork methods I guess that playworkers have to find out where their policies and practices originate and convince them that playwork has policies and practices which are just as valid, or even more so. Somehow we have to convince workers in other areas that, far from being optional, play is irreplaceable in all effective learning. My Indian friend Arvind Gupta introduced me to a lovely little Japanese story called Toto Chan; the little girl at the window. It tells how a very intelligent girl trapped in a classroom spent her time looking out at the landscape and ignored the lessons. The teacher realized what was wrong and made a deal with the children that, if they would carry out their classroom tasks in the morning, he would take them out into the surrounding forest to play in the afternoons. By this means the children's classwork improved by leaps and bounds as they discovered about the real world by direct experience.

Why are you optimistic about the future of play?
It is irrefutable that children will always play whatever their environment. A recent edition of the International Play Association (IPA) international journal PlayRights was entirely devoted to the lives of children in war-torn parts of the world. It showed that, even where their daily lives were at serious risk of death, they found ways of playing alone and with others to satisfy their inbuilt, inescapable need. But there is plenty of evidence that such children are badly damaged by their terrible experiences and are likely to learn to be aggressive by living with aggression, just as children who are constantly being criticized and judged in school tend to be critical and judgemental of others. So it is essential, I believe, that they have somewhere in their lives where they can learn at their own pace in settings where they can develop whatever interests absorb them. A good quality adventure playground will do this.

PHOTOS BY DONNE BUCK, CURATED BY MORGAN LEICHTER-SAXBY

Program Tour 231

Contemporary Adventure Playgrounds

While I enjoy working with schools and childcare settings to design and build natural playscapes I've also always been in love with adventure playgrounds and over the years I toured and visited sites across Europe any chance I could get. The first visits were mind blowing—crazy-looking kid-built scrap-wood structures, kids cooking over fires, bike-welding, huge gardens, living willow sculptures, farm animals wandering around, eating delicious homemade cauldron potato soup boiled on site. Good stuff! I loved seeing the amazing things the kids were doing in these places but what also amazed me was the fact that it was supported and sanctioned by the local adults—playworkers, parents, and government officials who all spoke passionately of the need for children to have access to nature, loose parts, farms, and freedom. These places felt like the ultimate environments for and by children and places that all children need access to— especially children living in over-protected societies. Here were places where kids were free to be kids and trusted to be safe, somewhat responsible, and get along with each other. In short, these were places that understood and respected childhood and children's rights. Inspiring!

Further visits reinforced these ideas and brought up new feelings in my heart about the need for these places back home. Fellow North Americans on these tours often commented that "*we could never do this back home*" because of lawsuits, safety, and liability (I suppose). Yet as I watched German children digging giant holes, tending sheep, pounding nails, and eating freshly picked fruits and vegetables I knew that these were *exactly* the kinds of environments that we needed back home, desperately! These European playground tours gave me great ideas and inspiration as a designer, but they also planted seeds of a desire to somehow, someday help start an adventure playground and help bring adventure play back to North America. We'll get to that germination a little bit later… but first how about a tour?

PHOTO BY MAGGIE FULLER

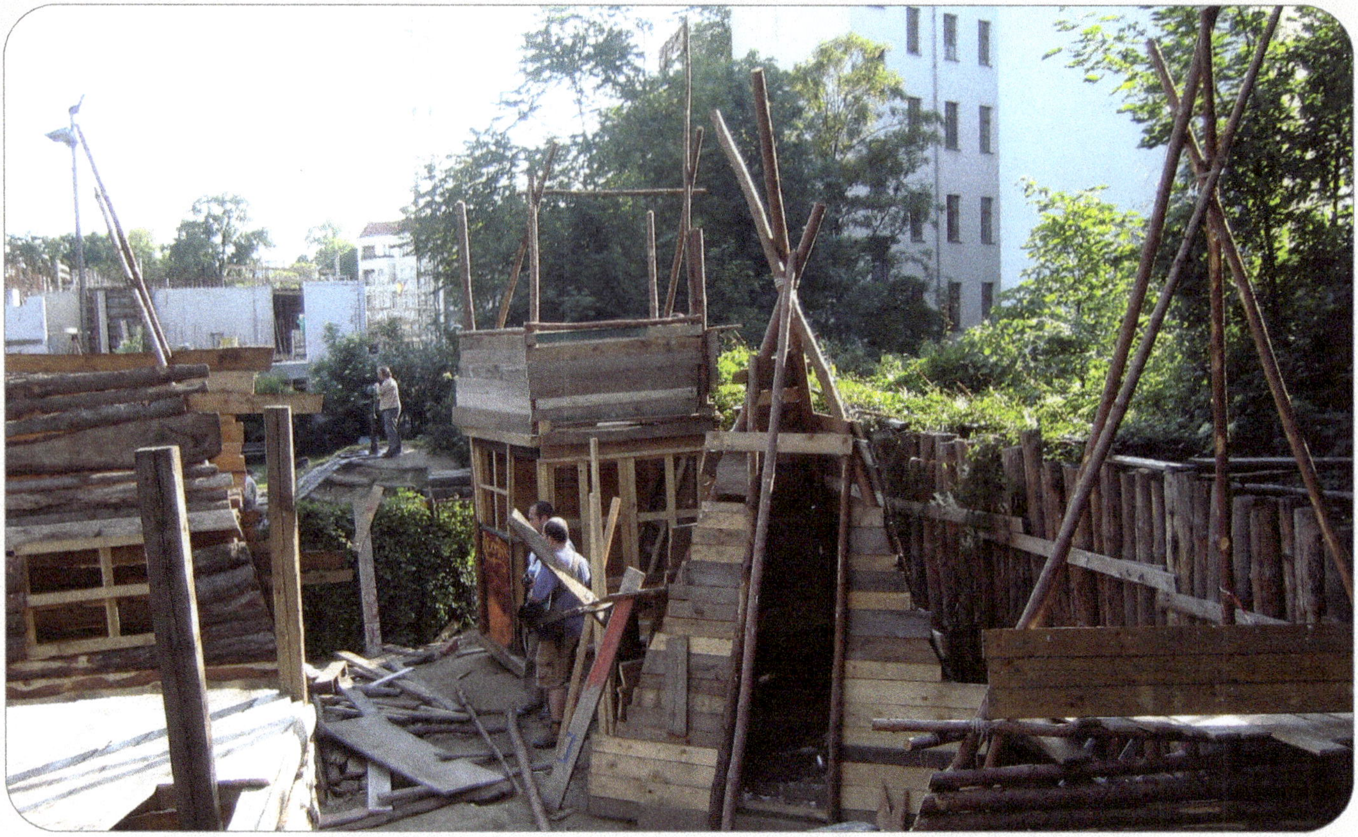

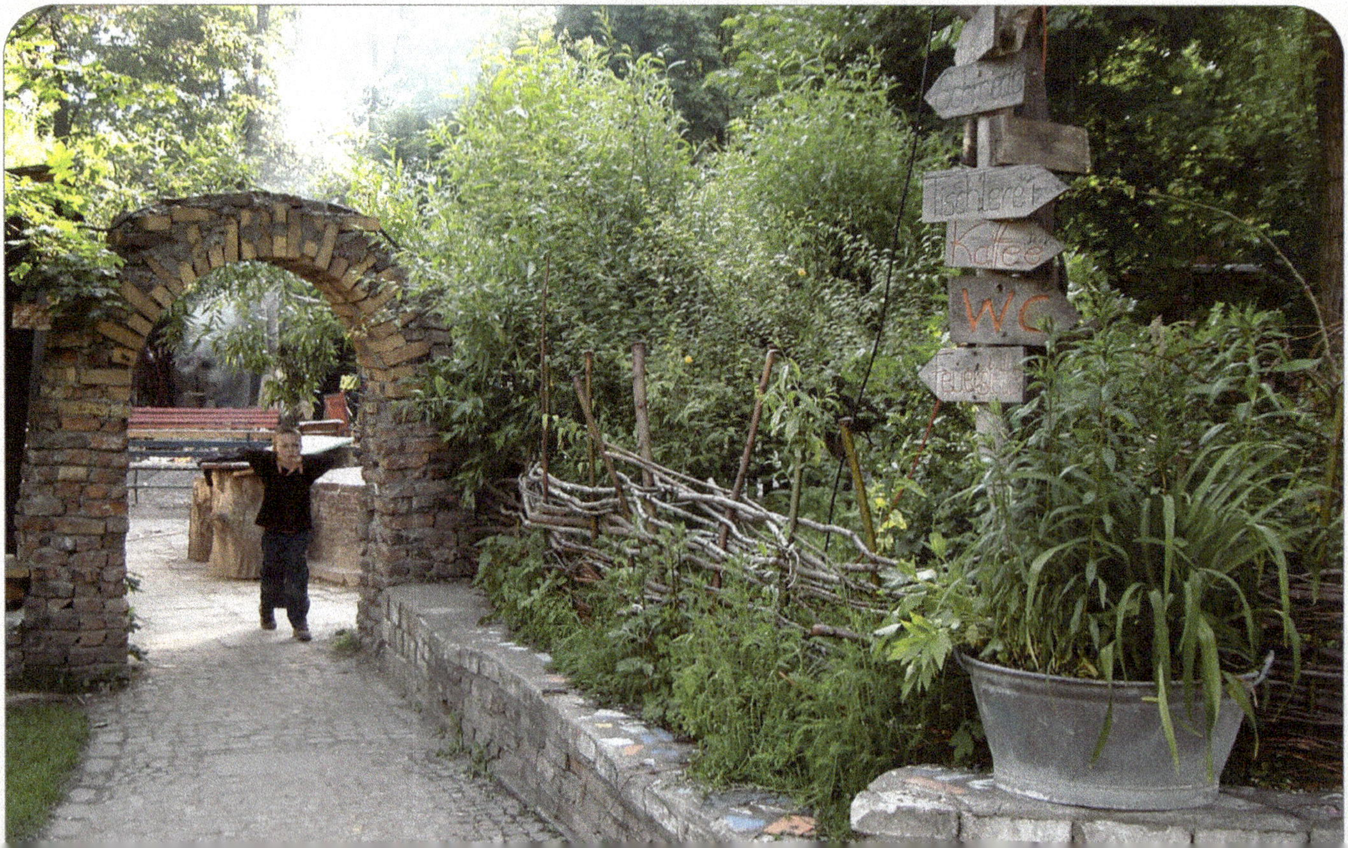
Tischlerei
Kafee
WC

Kolle 37

BERLIN, GERMANY

Some people go to Europe for the romance, the wine, the history, the architecture. I like that stuff too, but I also like going to Europe to tour adventure playgrounds. What can I say? Many European countries are committed to children's rights and I love seeing what they have done to support children's unstructured free play and connections to nature, even in the biggest cities.

One of my favorite stops over the years has been to Berlin, Germany to visit natural playscapes, adventure playgrounds, and urban farms. While the rest of Berlin feels quite organized with carefully planned details of development, parks, and transportation, these nature-filled rough and tumble environments for children seem kind of out of place…until you realize that they too have been carefully planned into the neighborhoods of Berlin's children and youth.

With a belief that children need to be connected to nature through gardens, orchards and animals, the Germans have built actual working farms right in the city center. I've visited urban farm and play spaces that were built where the Berlin Wall once stood, separating East from West. With the wall gone these spaces were opened up for everyone to enjoy, and keep gardens and collectively care for animals. Urban farms often have children's components built in with sand play, water features, and loose parts for play.

And then there are the amazing adventure playgrounds like this one in the Prenzlauer Berg district of Berlin: Kolle 37. Open since 1990 this space has an extensive area for hut-fort-den building with scrap lumber, hammers, saws, drills, ladders, and nails. It's truly incredible. The elaborate structures on site often take weeks or months to build. They are constantly getting scrap lumber replenished from local contractors who deliver it on site. Kids build, the structures grow, and every year or two when they are ready (so I was told) with the help of the fire department they light it all on fire and start fresh. Impressive.

When asked about safety and all the protuding nails sticking out everywhere our German playworker tour guide said that the majority of injuries happen to adults taking tours (!) and not the kids. The kids pounded in all the nails and they know what to look out for. The adult visitors do not! That does have some logic to it, I suppose. Kids also weave baskets, build with clay, repair bicycles, make metal sculpture in a real blacksmith forge, cook over fires and bake bread in their kid-built clay oven. Yeah!

One "shocking" moment for me (back when this sort of thing shocked me) was during the tour walking past a large bonfire…with nobody around. *Um, hello? Does anybody know there is a big fire burning here?* I waited for a while but nobody showed up. I kept going about the tour but circled back a few times to keep an eye on the fire. Still no one tending it. What was going on?! Then, sure enough, when the fire burned down a bit, out comes a boy with a large cast iron frying pan and three fat sausages in it. He bends down, checks the flames, then fries up his lunch over the fire. As the yummy smell filled the area I had a good chuckle to myself. Silly American. That's how you cook lunch.

The 3-acre playground is open every afternoon with trained, professional playworkers always on site, helping out around the edges as playworkers do. Kindergartens and school groups use the space in the mornings and their large clubhouse is used for cultural events and classes for the community after hours.

Program Tour 237

PHOTO BY DAVID SPENCER RAMSEY

The Land

WREXHAM, WALES

While The Land is a relatively new adventure playground for United Kingdom standards (started in 2011) it has been getting a lot of positive attention because it is considered by many in the play world to be a shining example of the authentic "old school" style of adventure playgrounds: less adult-built creations and more "junk." And if any adventure playground was thinking of returning to the early "Junk Playground" name and could pull it off with flair it would be The Land.

I mean, just look! There is indeed land (some nice mature trees, hills, even a small creek) but there is also junk, junk, glorious junk. Plastic tubes and pallets, graffiti, boards, buckets, old furniture, tubes, cushions, rope, kid-built zip lines and swings, giant spools, tires, mud, concrete tunnels, old mannequins, punching bags, metal storage units, and well, see for yourself! The Land is geared for children and young people aged 5-16 and says that it aims to provide a varied environment where children and young people can experience risk and challenge. The project is "open access" so children and young people are free to come and go as they please (another reason The Land is appreciated by adventure playground purists).

The Land is but one part of a larger playwork effort by the government-supported Play On Plas Madoc group that provides playworkers not only at The Land but also runs a "playranger" program called Street Play where playworkers visit the streets of the neighborhood each evening to support play where children live. The Inclusive Project provides support for children and young people who are unable to access any of the projects independently. Such good work. I am always amazed and inspired by the commitment to children and play by all levels of the Welsh government. We have so many great models to learn from!

Program Tour 241

PHOTOS BY DAVID SPENCER RAMSEY

Rødovre Byggelegeplads Adventure Playground
COPENHAGEN, DENMARK

It could very well be that Denmark—the birthplace of adventure playgrounds—has the best playgrounds in the world. The Danes have extensive parks and playground systems that incorporate nature, celebrate artistically-designed play equipment and staff full-time playworkers at public playgrounds. They have playful streets, plazas and sidewalks. So many things to be inspired by!

I had the chance to visit Copenhagen a few years ago and as usual when visiting countries that prioritize play and the needs of children my heart was opened and my mind was blown. I saw fantastical nature play parks built on reclaimed industrial property, respectfully designed early childhood nature playscapes, green public schoolyards, and my favorite: the Rødovre Byggelegeplads Adventure Playground.

Originally opened in 1964 this construction playground has been ever-expanding and is one of the largest "building playground" sites in Denmark today. Located in a suburban neighborhood outside of Copenhagen children walk or ride their bikes leisurely to the site after school or on weekends. As I walked around I was struck by how authentically and deeply the site was designed with children's interests and needs in mind. Staffed full-time by adult playworkers there was an enormous clubhouse with a kitchen to cook in, eating areas, computer rooms, an indoor stage for plays, play rooms, parrot cages and music rooms filled with electric guitars and drum sets. There were wild woodsy areas and a sports court that doubles as a skating rink every winter. There are horse riding stables, play equipment areas, in-ground trampolines, elaborate garden spaces, cooking fire pits, sculpture-making spaces, and building areas.

This place has kid-sized boulevards of kid-built scrap lumber treehouses, playhouses, platforms, dens, forts, and hideouts. I walked around amazed at the construction skills, the whimsical designs, and the fun colors of all the structures. Unlike the Kolle 37 in Berlin this playground had plenty of room to expand so they never tore down or burned up their creations. Instead they just built new avenues and continued to build out their child-sized city. There were literally decades worth of kid-built constructions with new creations being hammered together every day. It seemed to go on forever with new surprises around every corner.

As I stood marveling at the creations I suddenly noticed something: only half of the structures were built for

children. The other half were bunny hutches! Every child builds their own bunny hutch and takes care of a few bunnies, being responsible to feed, water and clean up after their bunnies. (When I visited they had a 200+ bunny population—and growing!) Besides bunnies they also cared for goats, pigs, roosters and hens. So awesome. This place was part camp, part farm, part kid society with adults helping out only when needed. It's the dream of what provision for play and childhood could look like if we knew we could care this much and dream this big. Turns out we can!

245

The Venny Adventure Playground

MELBOURNE, AUSTRALIA

"Risk Taking Playground—Shut Gate"...that sign says it all! Within this chainlink fence on the edge of a large public park sits a messy, risky, wild land for kids designed for fun, leisure, and shenanigans. Not as much of a "construction playground" as the other sites on our tour, this playground is filled with loose parts, weird materials, clever structures and an impressive garden (with chickens!). The energy-efficient clubhouse is a passive-solar green building made from steel shipping containers and the whole space has the feel of being designed by adults who really understand children's needs and interests. Rules for adults' behavior are posted on the front door while children build fires, blast off in imaginative space ships, make creations in messy mud kitchens, grow vegetables, laze in hammocks, play foosball, climb trees, hug chickens, and defy gravity on a set of in-ground trampolines!

Berkeley Adventure Playground

BERKELEY, CALIFORNIA

The Berkeley Adventure Playground has been going strong since opening in 1979. They held it down during the heyday of United States adventure playgrounds, kept it going through the lean years when they were listed as the only adventure playground in the country, and have helped inspire the new generation of Adventure Playgrounds popping up throughout North America. We owe a lot to their continued success and models of sustainability and grit.

More of a "destination playground" for families the Berkeley Adventure Playground feels like a vacant lot located by the waterfront area at the Berkeley Marina. The playground sports a giant zip line, art areas, weeds, cargo nets, sketchy climbing structures and towers, old boats, and a massive amount of construction and paint materials for children to build and create with. The playground is designed for children seven years old and older, but younger children are welcome as long as they are "within arms reach" of a participating adult.

PHOTOS BY SHARON DANKS

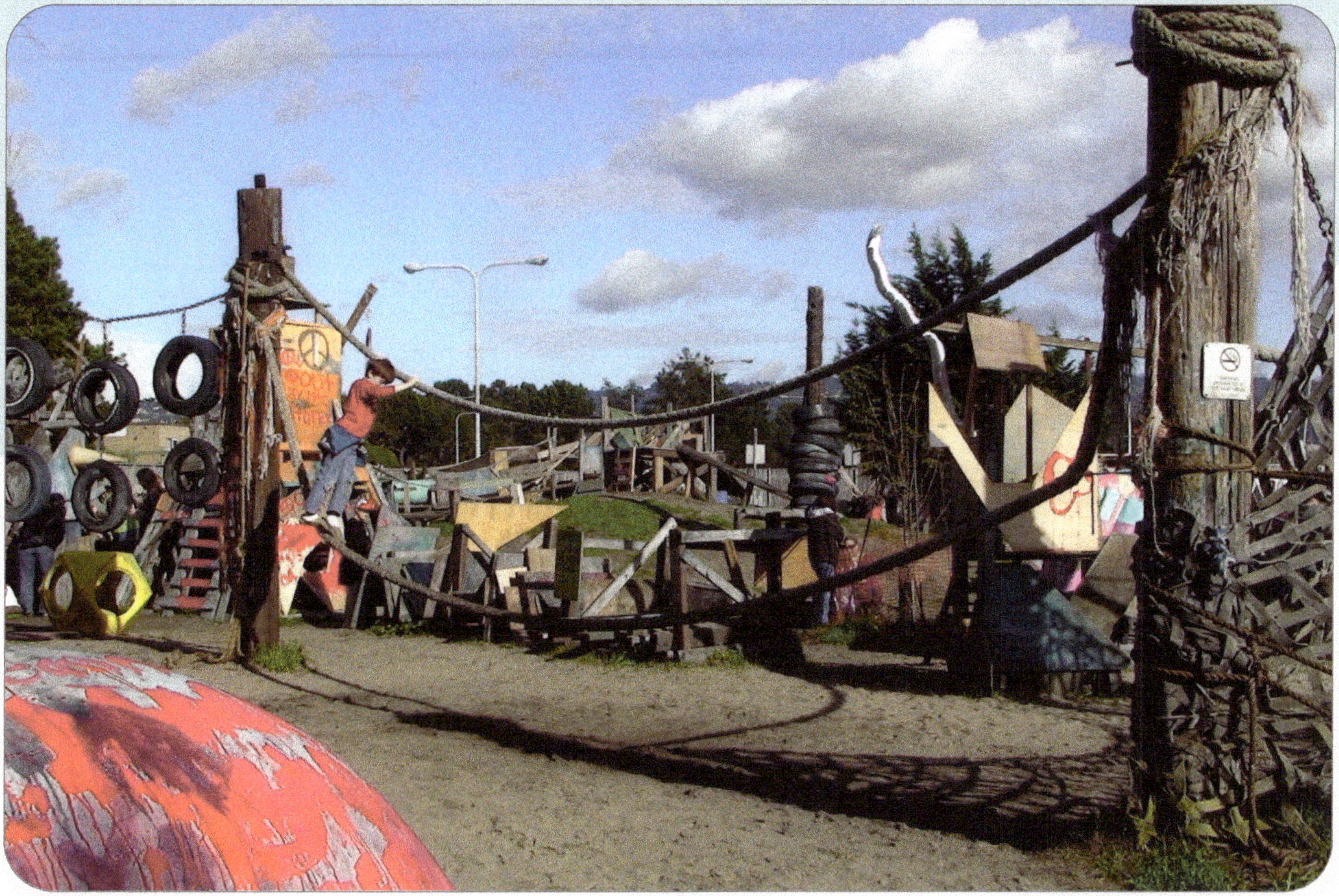

You
be 6 or
older to
ride the
trolley

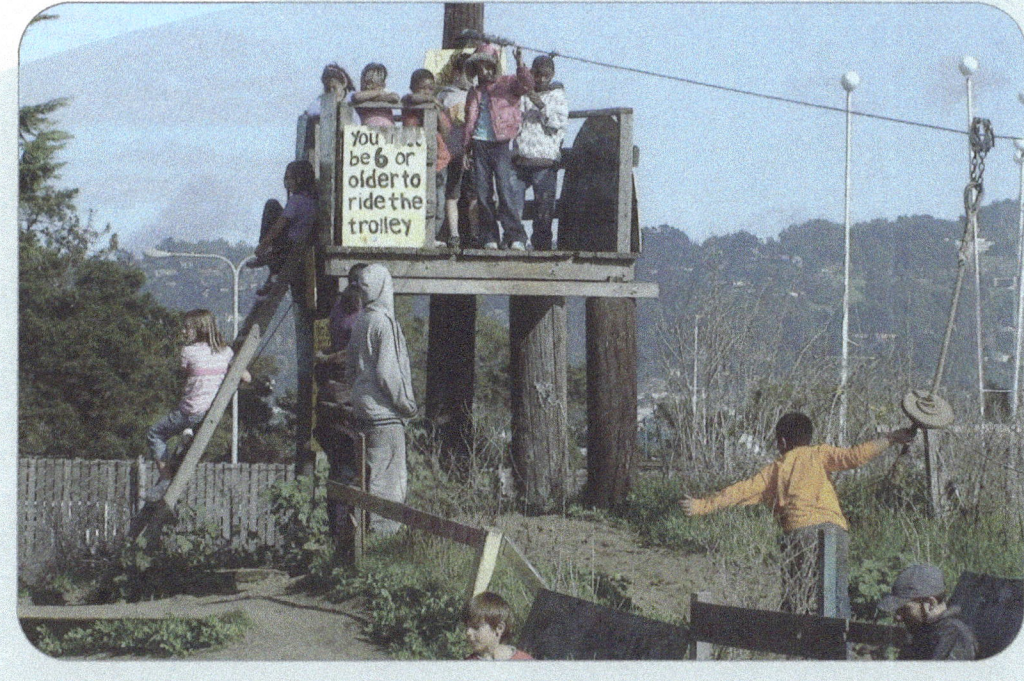

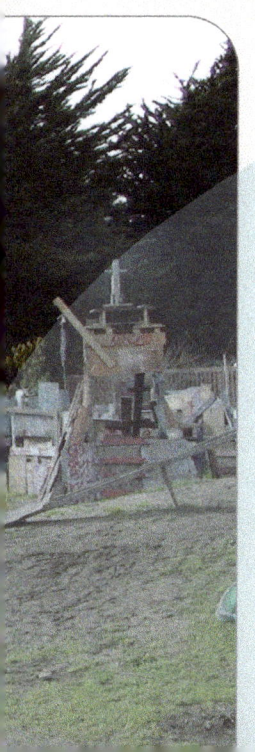

I like their response to the question of what children should wear when they visit:

Everyone must wear sturdy shoes like tennis shoes, NOT flip flops, sandals, crocs or clogs. Stepping on a nail is a possibility and sturdy shoes protect feet. Wear clothes that can get dirty, wet, painted on and you may consider bringing a change of clothes for wet or muddy days. Warning: Our playground paint is water-based tempera and may not come out of clothing even with pre-treating.

Sounds like good advice to me. Be prepared and bring on the risky mess!

PHOTOS BY SHARON DANKS

Hands-on-Nature Anarchy Zone

ITHACA, NEW YORK

One of my favorite places in the world is the Hands-on-Nature Anarchy Zone (HONAZ) at Ithaca Children's Garden (ICG). Supported by the US Fish and Wildlife Service and fully inspired by adventure playgrounds, HONAZ is a place where children are free to dig in the dirt, climb trees, build forts, make their own swings, play with water and a million other things.

Located on city parkland, HONAZ and Ithaca Children's Garden are open every day and free to the public. School-age children visit during field trips, preschools spend whole days on site, afterschool programs bring van loads of kids to the space, and the summer camp program hires trained playworkers to support child-directed play at HONAZ and the garden as a whole. Special events like International Mud Day and the Festival of Fire and Ice bring thousands of participants out for spectacular fun. Yet on the average day it is children and their families visiting the space on their own to have fun, get messy, and do what they want to do. From the moment children see the "Anarchy Zone" they know that it is a place for kids and a place where they can be free to play however they want to. Parents are encouraged to join in the fun, yes, but also to stand back, watch their children play, and be amazed.

I had the pleasure of being a part of the team who initiated the project and got it off the ground. US Fish and Wildlife Service provided seed money for a shed and loose materials and a grant from Cornell University supported our initial staff training. Pop-up Adventure Play led the training of staff in playwork and Alex Cote was hired to be the first official playworker. While adventure playgrounds of Europe had traditionally been supported by tax dollars, HONAZ grew out of local, grassroots support—mostly material and in-kind donations. We used the community-built model and did it ourselves with help from our friends. Local lumberyards donated scrap wood, service stations provided used tires, a country club gave us buckets of used golf balls, the University climbing wall donated used climbing rope that they were done with, a sailing club gave us old sails, and our city forester delivered a mountain of wood chips and huge tree stumps. A true community effort! There are always businesses and individuals who want to help with projects like these ("*this is how I played when I was a kid!*"). All you have to do is ask.

The space has become much loved locally and regionally. I have a fun memory of over-hearing a mom at the grocery store telling a friend, *"You've got to come over to our house, we built an anarchy zone in our backyard!"* That's the spirit! Saying yes to play. Saying yes to mess. We can all do it. It doesn't have to be big. Start small, and keep it going.

Introducing Early Childhood Centers

And here we have what I would call "best practice" early childhood outdoor play settings. Yes! These centers have it all: nature, loose parts, tools, art, water, mud, mess, and most importantly of all: adults like you who love play, respect children, and have found a million ways to say "yes" to play. The spaces aren't always pretty and never pristine, but every center you see here is a shining example of what we can do in the real world when we put our minds and intentions to creating true open-ended environments for children. You can imagine what the untrained eye might think of places that look like this: Anarchy!

But we know what's really going on. The play is amazing, the possibilities unlimited, and it's all because the adults in charge have made it their mission to support play in all its wild ways. These are people just like you. They all have budgets and comfort zones, and staff with different feelings toward risk. They all deal with licensing and parents who may feel uncomfortable with saying "yes" to play or who need extra guidance to understand this vision of excellence. But they are working within the current system and making it happen.

We all have beliefs in our hearts. We all have our ideas of the worlds we want to create for children. It's not always easy to manifest our dreams, but it's always possible. Little by little, step by step. Nothing happens overnight and everything is a process. But it can all happen, if you start small, work slowly, build consensus, and learn as you go. These are all the skills that give us strength and help us reach our goals.

The following environments are some of my favorite places in the world for children. They are not fancy or funded by the Danish or German government. But they have all the qualities that I believe children need, deserve, and love: time, space, materials, and supportive adults that say yes to child-directed play. Yes!

PHOTO COURTESY OF TAKOMA PARK COOP

Canterbury Community Nursery School

RICHMOND, VIRGINIA

Look at this place. What a mess. I love it! It's all happening here: mud, sand, boards, water, hills, loose stuff, and challenge. Hard to believe that only a few years ago this rough and tumble space was a regular yard here at Canterbury. It's certainly not now. Somewhere along the line staff sparked the idea to dedicate one of their fenced-in yards to the spirit of messy adventure play and there was no turning back (and no more grass—but what's wrong with that, right?). An adventurous space doesn't need to be gigantic and it doesn't have to be your whole outdoor environment. That's what I like so much about this spot. It's just one of Canterbury's fenced-in outdoor play spaces. Their other yards have swings and playhouses and other regular fixed play equipment. That's fine. But lo and behold they now also have one of the coolest open-ended, child-directed, adventure playground-inspired spaces around. Trials and errors happen here. Grand creations are built and destroyed. Hills climbed, obstacles conquered, lessons learned. What happens when we adults turn over our yards to children's ideas and aesthetics? This! How sweet it is…

PHOTOS COURTESY OF CANTERBURY COMMUNITY NURSERY SCHOOL

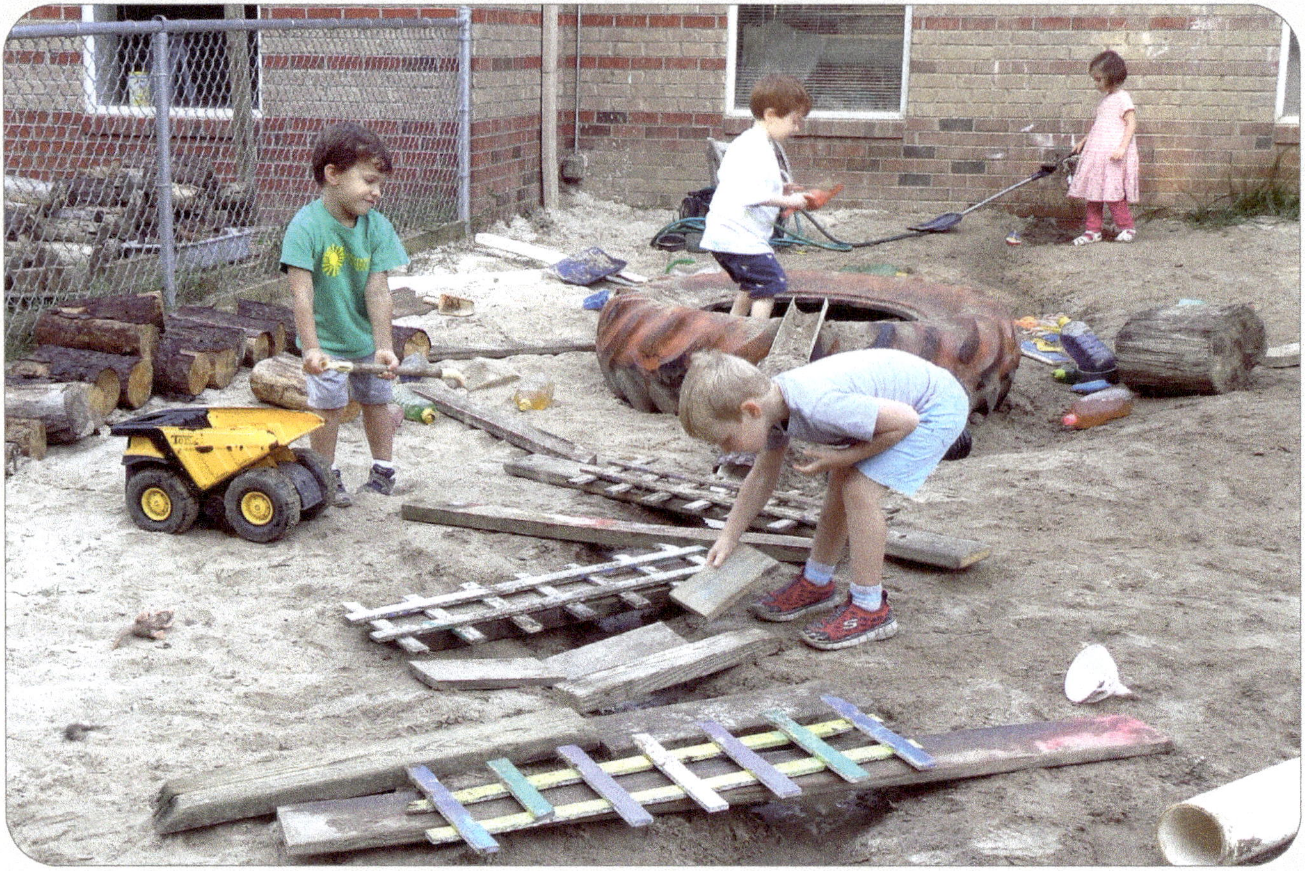

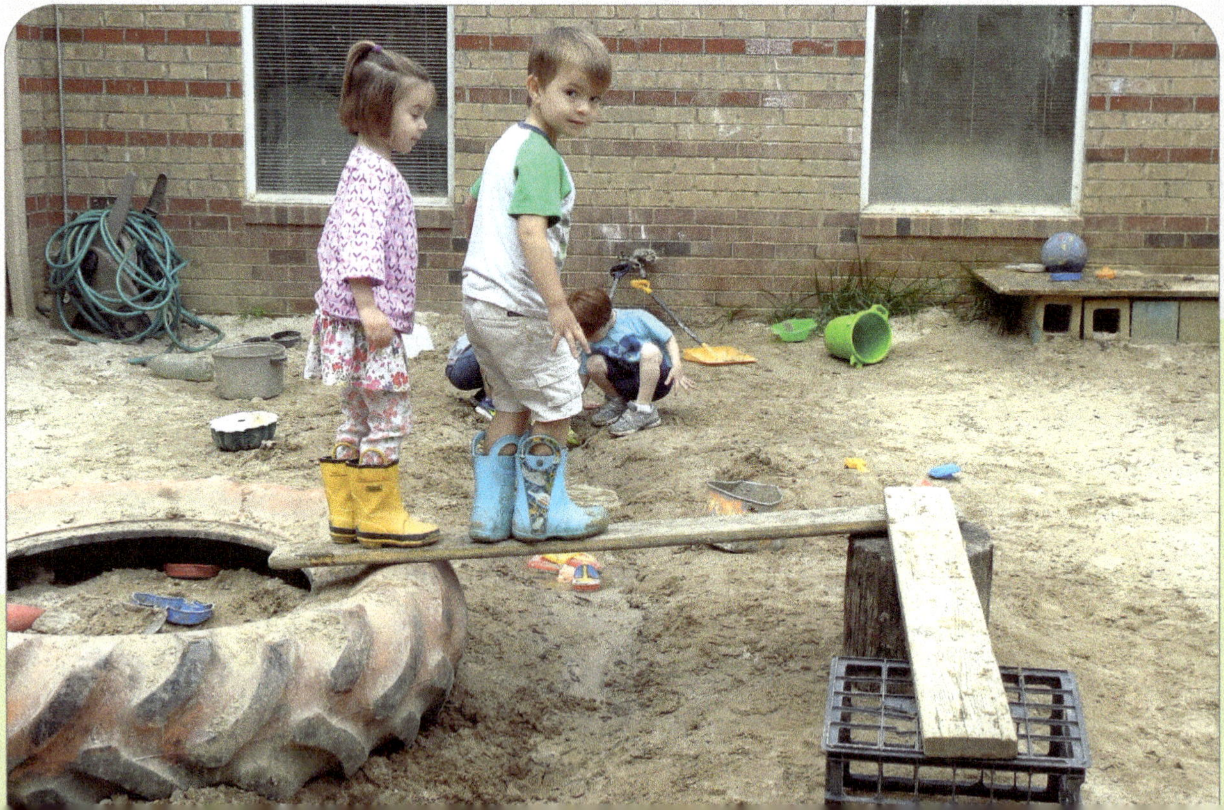

Program Tour 263

PHOTOS COURTESY OF CANTERBURY COMMUNITY NURSERY SCHOOL

Takoma Park Cooperative Nursery School

TAKOMA PARK, MARYLAND

You can tell amazing things happen in this yard. Gutsy things too, like children with fire and children on shed roofs. And how about this variety of loose parts these children have at their fingertips? Cool stuff! It ain't all pretty but it's certainly all beautiful, that's for sure. Sticks, bricks, vacuum cleaner tubes. Beauty is in the eye of the beholder. I guess this is what things looks like when children are doing the beholding!

PHOTOS COURTESY OF TAKOMA PARK COOP

PHOTOS COURTESY OF TAKOMA PARK COOP

Program Tour 267

PHOTOS COURTESY OF TAKOMA PARK COOP

Corner Of The Sky

ITHACA, NEW YORK

Behold, one of my favorite backyards anywhere. Both my sons have gone through this program and I love it so much—the yard makes me happy every time I see it. There is always something interesting going on and even if there are no children outside you can tell it's been a happening place. It's always different, always changing. Most people walking down the street would never know it's there but behind the friendly blue house sits an alternate reality for play, living and being. It's creatively wild, democratic, nurturing and loving. Children can really stretch out and grow. Bare feet, outdoor snack, loose materials, water play, sand box meetings and more. Oh to be a preschooler at Corner of the Sky!

Program Tour 271

Discovery Early Learning Center

POOLESVILLE, MARYLAND

I can't say enough how cool I think this yard is. I mean look at it: have they ever mown their grass? I don't think so. It's the best! This is what grass is supposed to look like (especially if you ask grass). It's also what early childhood centers can look like when they push past the pressure of yards looking tidy or proper in the eyes of adults. Is it a vacant lot? A junkyard? A risky environment for children? Yep. I showed some of these pictures once to a group of licensing regulators and they stopped me to ask if I was saying this was good or bad. I said "good!" and they said, "oh, ok" and we continued with the presentation. They ended up loving it too and seeing the deep value of an environment like this. The old way of looking at yards in quick sweeping glances might discount a place like this as inappropriate or dangerous or something. But now when we take more careful looks and reflect on children's true play needs we see that a space like this is a living, breathing child's habitat overflowing with wildness and life and magical possibilities for play, creation, imagination, challenge, risk, everything. I say it's a little slice of adventure play heaven…

PHOTOS BY KISHA REID

274   Adventures in Risky Play

PHOTOS BY KISHA REID

PHOTOS BY KISHA REID

Reimagining Recess

Elementary schools are getting in on the loose parts playwork fun too and looking at ways to loosen recess rules, create more freedom and choice, sprinkle in risk, and say yes to play. While United Kingdom organizations like Outdoor Play and Learning (OPAL) and ScrapStore Play Pods have worked with hundreds of elementary schools throughout England to bring risky play, loose parts, and playwork principles to recess we are just starting to crack the code here in North America. That's ok. You've got to start sometime!

As a part of the Just Play Project I've had the fun of helping to expand recess possibilities at public elementary schools in my hometown Ithaca, New York. When we approached some local schools about trying a pilot program, the answer right away was yes! My son's principal was immediately all for it. She grew up in a creative alternative school and had been a teacher and coordinator of the PreK program for the district. She understood play and the need for more freedom and opportunities to encounter risk in a safe nurturing environment—a school. Other schools followed. Soon grants were written and awarded and we were off to the races!

We bought storage sheds for our two schools, purchased and procured donations of loose part play materials and dove into staff trainings looking at rules, adults roles, and introducing playwork principles into recess monitoring. We hired trained playworkers to assist the staff in day-to-day support of the play. Success!

It's a process for sure to change hearts and minds about what play at recess should look like. These schools had been doing things quite differently for a long time. But with meetings, honest dialogue, group consensus building, support and problem-solving, staff have been able to reassess their roles. While they may have been hesitant at first, once they saw the positive and surprising effects on children's play many have become vocal supporters of the project. Some have felt a sense of relief to be able to allow "kids to be kids" and have enjoyed being less of a watchdog and more of a supporter of the children's ideas and play. From the start the staff reported seeing much more creative play, collaborative play, and play that was much more inclusive of other children than before the introduction of loose parts.

Program Tour 279

Each school used to have a long list of rules that were strictly enforced. Now they have boiled it down to three: *take care of yourself, take care of others, and take care of the stuff*. There are plenty of logistics to deal with and continual conversations among staff about implementation, but we are well on our way on our recess journey to make child-directed play a reality for all ages of children. It's not just for preschoolers—big kids need stuff too!

Program Tour 281

there is no conclusion

just new beginnings

what happens next depends on you

Conclusion

Well, what new ideas did you have reading this book? Did you have any "aha" moments? What are reflections on your own work with children? What are your new aspirations?

Were there scenes in here that resonated with you? Any ideas that match your own? It can be helpful to hear them again in a book, reinforcing your thoughts and feelings. It can also be like giving you permission to try new things. *You can do this, give it a try.*

You can let go and trust your children to find their way through new situations. You have the gumption to stand up for play and this way of being with children. *"By golly, that's it, I'm changing!"* Then you start to have conversations with others about risky play, sharing stories and rewards. And little by little, change happens. It's beautiful, fun, and inspiring—for your children and for you.

Remember, the question isn't when are you going to have dangerous tools for your children outside. The question is: What's the first *little* change you can try? What's the *smallest* thing you can do? I say the first little change you can make is inside you. How do you think and feel about risky play? Where is your own growing edge? What's your first step for action?

It's all about taking those deep breaths in the moment. *"What is my yes or no?"* Trust the child. Trust yourself. Breathe and watch. Instead of stepping forward, take a step back and observe what is really happening. Is it chaos? Freedom? Both? The world probably isn't falling apart even if sometimes you want to cover your eyes. New space can open for you in the moment and new reasons to try it again.

Little by little, breath by breath, you'll see things happening that feel better than before: a puddle jump, balancing on a log, even climbing up a slide. *"Oh, that actually worked,"* you'll exhale and say. *"Let's try that again. I'll let them do something else, a little more."* And a little more, a little more, a little more, and a little more. Until you've exercised that *"yes"* part of yourself so much you realize, *"oh, this is who I am now. Yes, I keep an eye on my children. I watch them carefully. But I can also stretch my comfort zone and grow my ability to say yes to play."* You can still say no anytime you need to. But the goal is to say yes more. Helping you get there was the goal of this book. Good luck!

Say yes to play.

Ready to explore the topic even further? Go to page 295.

PART 5
Extra Stuff

Risk-Benefit Analysis

Here's your very own Risk Benefit Analysis (RBA) form to scan, copy, print and fill out. While there are far more detailed and thorough versions you can find online that may better suit your purposes in the long run, this simple form can start you on your way to weighing risks with benefits and devising management strategies to minimize injuries. Fill them out and keep them on file to show parents and authorities your thoughtful approach to risky play. What's the first activity you're going to RBA analyze with this?

BENEFITS	RISKS

Risk-Benefit Analysis

MANAGEMENT

NOTES

End Notes

1. Ben Dalby and Courtney Gardner, Free for All Baltimore, A child-led community building project. https://www.freeforallbaltimore.org/post/an-open-letter-to-u-s-advocates-for-play, (accessed 1 May 2020).

2. Michael Yogman, Andrew Garner, Jeffrey Hutchinson, Kathy Hirsh-Pasek, Roberta Michnick Golinkoff, "The Power of Play: A Pediatric Role in Enhancing Development in Young Children." *Pediatrics,* September 2018, 142 (3).

3. Ellen Beate Hansen Sandseter, "Categorizing Risky Play - How Can We Identify Risk-Taking In Children's Play?" *European Early Childhood Education Research Journal,* 2007, 15(2), p.237-252.

4. Ibid.

5. Ibid.

6. Astrid Lindgren and Ingrid Vang Nyman, *Pippi Moves In*. Stockholm, Sweden: Raben & Sjorgren Agency, 2012.

7. Playwork Principles Scrutiny Group, *The Playwork Principles*, Cardiff, UK: The Playwork Foundation: 2005.

8. Charlotte Ringsmose, Grethe Kragh-Müller, "Nordic Social Pedagogical Approach to Early Years" *International Perspectives on Early Childhood Education and Development, Book 15*. New York, NY: Springer, 2016.

9. Sam Nicholson, "Theory of Loose Parts: How Not To Cheat Children" *Landscape Architect Journal,* October 1971, p.30-34.

10. Australian Early Childhood Guide, "Guide to the National Quality Framework," *National Quality Framework Resource Kit*, Australian Children's Education and Care Quality Authority, 2013.

11. Warden. C., *Nature Pedagogy: The Art of Being with Nature Inside, Outside and Beyond*. PhD thesis. Liverpool, UK: Liverpool Hope University, 2018.

12. Gill. T. *No Fear: Growing Up in a Risk Averse Society*. London, UK: Calouste Gulbenkian Foundation, 2007.

13. Emilian Geczi, Monica Wiedel-Lubinski, Megan Gessler, Kit Harrington, Kendall Becherer, "Nature Preschools and Kindergartens at Record Numbers in the US." Washington, DC: Natural Start Alliance, 2017.

14. Luisa Olivera and Robert Steck, *Building an Adventure Playground in Cambridge, Findings and Recommendations,* Cambridge, MA: City of Cambridge, 2014, p.10.

Resource List
Look these up for inspiration!

PLAY ORGANIZATIONS
Play England
Play Wales
Play London
Play Scotland

IPA (International Play Association)
US Play Coalition
Alliance for Childhood
TASP - (Association for the Study of Play)
World Forum Foundation

Child and Nature Network
Green School Yards America
Child and Nature Alliance

KaBOOM!
Playground Ideas
Just Play Project

ADVENTURE PLAYGROUNDS
play:groundNYC
Glammis Adventure Playground
Santa Clarita Valley Adventure Play
KOOP Adventure Play

PLAYWORK
Pop-up Adventure Play
Playwork Primer
Playwork Foundation

SCHOOL-AGE PLAY
OPAL
Scrap Store Play Pods

RISKY PLAY
OutsidePlay.ca
Ellen Beate Hansen Sandseter
Risk Benefit Assessment for Outdoor Play: a Canadian Tool Kit

CHILD-FRIENDLY CITY
Unicef Child Friendly Cities Initiative
8-80 Cities
Child in the City Foundation

PLAY FILMS
The Land
Where Do the Children Play?
Nature Play

NATURE PLAY DESIGN
Rusty Keeler play design
Bienenstock Playgrounds
Nature Explore
Earthscapes

PLAY BLOGS
Rethinking Childhood
Playgroundology
Play Everything
Peter Gray

BOOKS
Free Range Kids by Lenore Skenazy
Design Build Play by Robin Christie
Nature Play at Home by Nancy Striniste
Natural Playscapes by Rusty Keeler
Seasons of Play by Rusty Keeler
Balanced and Barefoot by Angela Hanscom
Let the Children Play by Pasi Sahlberg & William Doyle
Free to Learn by Peter Gray
Playing it Up edited by Joan Almon
Savage Park by Amy Fusselman
Children's Participation by Roger Hart
Asphalt to Ecosystems by Sharon Danks

Rusty's Risky Play Class
rustykeeler.com

Locations

Thanks to the schools who helped make this book!

EUROPE

Auchlone Nature Kindergarten
Crieff, Scotland
page 186

Kolle 37
Berlin, Germany
page 235

The Land
Wrexham, Wales
page 239

New Ark Adventure Playground
& City Farm
Peterborough, United Kingdom
page 228

Rødovre Byggelegeplads Adventure
Playground
Copenhagen, Denmark
page 242

Swedish
Open-Air School
Malmo, Sweden
page 212

NORTH AMERICA

Adventure School
Ithaca, New York, United States
page 204

Berkeley Adventure
Playground
Berkeley, California, United States
page 250

Canterbury Community
Nursery School
Richmond, Virginia, United States
page 260

Child Central Station Group
Home Daycare
Marquette, Michigan, United States
page 162

Corner Of The Sky
Ithaca, New York, United States
page 268

Discovery Early Learning Center
Poolesville, Maryland, United States
page 272

Hands-On-Nature Anarchy Zone
Ithaca, New York, United States
page 254

Hudson Valley Sudbury School
Woodstock, New York, United States
page 216

Nelson Waldorf School
Nelson, British Columbia, Canada
page 61

St. David's Center for Child
and Family Development
Minnetonka Mills,
Minnesota, United States
page 142

Takoma Park Cooperative
Nursery School
Takoma Park, Maryland, United
States
page 264

OCEANIA

Beyond the Fence
Perth, Australia
page 30

Children's Programs
and Child Care Services
The University of British Columbia
(UBC)
Vancouver, British Columbia, Canada
page 160

Open Spaces Preschool
Whangarei, New Zealand
page 114, 199

The Point Preschool
Sydney, Australia
page 154

The Venny Adventure Playground
Melbourne, Australia
page 246

Rusty Keeler

Rusty Keeler lives beside a creek with his family in Ithaca, New York.

Rusty spent his childhood playing and his adult life designing for play.

Rusty's dream is for ALL children to have the freedom + time, space, and materials to play.

Learn more about Rusty at **rustykeeler.com**

So where do you go from here?

rustykeeler.com

Visit **rustykeeler.com** to learn more about Rusty's online classes, design consulting, public speaking, play products, workshops, newsletter and more!

RISKY PLAY ONLINE CLASS

You've read the book—you've seen the pictures—now delve deeper into your thinking about risky play with an in-depth online class created by author Rusty Keeler.

Rusty's Risky Play Class is chocked full of thoughtful questions, activities, videos, pictures, and loads of more bonus material that wouldn't fit in this book. Dig deep, imagine taking things to the next level and help your organization say YES more to play!

This class is great for individuals and organizations looking to be guided through the thought process of change.